Praise for
Everyone Wins!

Building a shared vocabulary of non-competitive games
and team challenges has been a critical element in building
our school culture. In addition to playing together with
a spirit of collaboration rather than competition, our
teachers find that de-briefing after playing these games
gives us rich fodder to explore group dynamics. I still use
my old coffee-stained copy with kids all the time!

—Paul Freedman, Head of School, Salmonberry and President,
SelfDesign Graduate University

Everyone Wins is a must-have resource for educators,
business leaders, camp staff and even family members
who recognize that cooperation doesn't just happen on its
own but that it can be nurtured and enhanced with
practice, intention and a good measure of fun.
Here you'll find a treasure trove of carefully selected
activities that build trust, empathy and team building
skills in a wonderfully clear and easy to follow manner.
In a world beset with conflict, social unrest and tension,
learning how to get along with one another has
never been more timely or necessary.

—Jacob Rodenburg, co-author,
The Big Book of Nature Activities

Everyone Wins is one of my favorite books
[by the Lumours]. I used it so much when I was
running children/family programs.

—Danelle Benstead Till, education specialist,
Alliance Charter Academy

...I have used the concepts, group processes and cooperative games [the Luvmours] teach in my work with my family, with teams, corporations, and our board of directors. Their work is life changing and Josette and Ba approach people and groups with passion and heart, as well as the "kid" in themselves.

—Jan Green Bernau, Project and Staff Development Manager, Willamette Valley Vineyards

I never realized just how cooperative activities could have so many uses.

—Melissa Faith, 5th grade teacher, Chico, CA

While our goal is to include the students in curriculum design it is difficult to satisfy the needs of the whole class. I used to find the process time-consuming and sometimes contentious. Now we just use the Values Clarification games and cooperative communication activities, (amended by the students) and success comes quickly.

—Jake Sensibol, 6th-7th grade teacher, Independent School

EVERYONE Wins!

COOPERATIVE GAMES & ACTIVITIES FOR ALL AGES

Revised and updated 3rd edition

Josette & Ba Luvmour

new society
PUBLISHERS

Cover design by Diane McIntosh.
Cover image: © iStock 489254336

Activity Level images: © iStock 478587008; © iStock 152136572;
© iStock 503671761; © iStock 98044988; © iStock 638620778.

Printed in Canada. First printing April 2019.

First edition copyright © 1990 by Josette and Sambhava Luvmour. Second edition copyright © 2007 by Josette and Sambhava Luvmour.

Inquiries regarding requests to reprint all or part of *Everyone Wins!* should be addressed to New Society Publishers at the address below. To order directly from the publishers, please call toll-free (North America) 1-800-567-6772, or order online at www.newsociety.com

Any other inquiries can be directed by mail to:
New Society Publishers
P.O. Box 189, Gabriola Island, BC V0R 1X0, Canada
(250) 247-9737

LIBRARY AND ARCHIVES CANADA CATALOGUING IN PUBLICATION

Luvmour, Josette, author
      Everyone wins! : cooperative games & activities for all ages /
Josette & Ba Luvmour. -- Revised and updated 3rd edition.

Includes index.
Issued in print and electronic formats.
ISBN 978-0-86571-902-6 (softcover).--ISBN 978-1-55092-695-8
(PDF).--ISBN 978-1-77142-291-8 (EPUB)

      1. Group games. 2. Cooperativeness in children. 3. Games.
I. Luvmour, Ba, 1947-, author II. Title.
GV1203.L88 2019   796.1   C2018-906365-3
                                        C2018-906366-1

Funded by the Government of Canada   Financé par le gouvernement du Canada

New Society Publishers' mission is to publish books that contribute in fundamental ways to building an ecologically sustainable and just society, and to do so with the least possible impact on the environment, in a manner that models this vision.

FSC MIX Paper from responsible sources FSC® C016245 www.fsc.org

Certified B Corporation

new society PUBLISHERS

Contents

Activity Level One

Activity Level Two

Activity Level Three

Activity Level Four

Activity Level Five

To Amber

For the Spirit in which she comes to play

Introduction to the First Edition

THERE WAS BIG TROUBLE ON THE PLAYGROUND at a local independent school. Violence was present almost every day, and most of the first and second grade children had formed cliques. The parent who had the responsibility for monitoring the playground was getting angrier and angrier and lacked support for coping with the situation. The teachers acknowledged the problem and saw it as an extension of difficulties in the classroom, but their every attempt to help backfired. Some parents blamed other parents and other children for the problem, and the administration and other teachers were growing increasingly alarmed. It was at this point that we were called in. Was there any way to relieve the pressure short of major surgery?

Since this is an introduction to cooperative games and activities, we won't describe in detail the different means used to ease the tensions at this school. Cooperative games and activities weren't sufficient unto themselves, but they were the critical factor. They not only provided a common ground for all to meet on but allowed us to test the effectiveness of the other conflict-resolution techniques being employed. The games served both diagnostic and remedial purposes.

The first time we met the class on the playground, we had them play "Spaghetti." This was our way of saying to them that we are all interconnected and, though sometimes relationships become knotted up, it is possible to find a solution. "Spaghetti" is played by having everyone stand in a circle, then each person taking the hand of someone not directly next to them. Each person must be holding the hand of two different people. The object is to recreate the circle while continuing to hold hands. This is not easy to do, and there is often no way to do it, but communication and patience are emphasized if there is to be any chance at all. Once children get the idea, they want very much to have success. This class played twice, with manners no one would have believed possible, before finally "winning."

Next we played "Rolling Along." In this game, children pair off, lie on their backs, and try to roll down a field with their toes connected. At first we let them pick their own partners; then we chose partners randomly; and finally we deliberately matched certain students together. Of course, there was dissatisfaction with both the random and deliberate methods of pairing, but the game was so much fun, and the release of energy so significant, that the children cooperated.

Then it was into group games such as "Chase in the Ocean" and "True or False." Then we collectively made an obstacle course and collectively navigated it. Finally we played "Hug a Tree." This was an important moment in the day because this game requires a high degree of trust. Children are in pairs and one is blindfolded. Then, in a fairly dense wood, the sighted child leads the blindfolded partner to a tree by a circuitous route. The blindfolded child explores the tree with all senses but sight. Then, via a different route, the child is led back to start, the blindfold removed, and the child tries to find the tree.

But how to arrange the pairs? If we put together children who had been having difficulty with one another and they violated trust, it was altogether likely that cooperative games would not be energized into healing intensity. If, on the other hand, we allowed the "best friends" who formed the core of the cliques to pair off, then there was the probability that those cliques would be reinforced.

The understanding of how the students were connected had been developing in us during the time the previous games were played. We relied on no other person's judgment, not even that of the teacher. It is in the course of the games, while involvement is total, that the child will forget the more superficial aspects of image and will react according to needs. For instance, two boys who were often the object of one another's aggression had greatly enjoyed being paired in the game "Rolling Along." They moved across the field so quickly that the other children were delighted and stopped to watch them. Everyone was surprised — and comfortable — when they realized the new roles these boys were living.

In every group there are those who have the capability of providing a "neutralizing" influence. Often, this capability is hidden, for there is great pressure to join one side or another. In this class of first and second graders, the neutralizers were well underground. Communication and "safe space" had deteriorated to that extent. But we had spotted them during the group games. They played the games for the enjoyment of it and did not worry who was next to them. They looked to us for information as to how best to play, and they were not afraid of telling those who interfered to be quiet.

The biggest clue to the identity of the neutralizers was their need to let us know they were not identified with any one group of children. They let us know in subtle and not-so-subtle ways. One child would deliberately stand apart from the group while awaiting the next round of play. Another would deliberately join in with a child or group she didn't usually join and would give us a verbal sign that she was doing so.

The neutralizers played a critical role in the games that followed. We split the more closely attached of the cliques among the neutralizers. The rest we arranged so that they were with children they weren't ordinarily with or ones with whom they had moderate difficulties. It worked out very well. By now our allotted time was spent, and it was with a groan of displeasure that the children returned to the classroom.

Over the next few weeks, we trained the parent who was in charge of the playground. Gradually, more and more complex games were introduced, each time expanding the children's perception of safe space. Eventually we played games like "Cast Your Vote" and "Interview," in which they could express their understanding of their classroom and their ideas of what they would like it to be. To do so took great courage on their part, and an open expression of courage was not readily forthcoming. There were other difficulties in the relationship of the classroom teacher and the parents, but finally the class reached a place where, at least in the playground, the children could channel their energy into cooperation.

Principles of Application

Cooperative games are a tool, and like all tools, they must be used with skill and sensitivity. One of the beautiful and exciting aspects of cooperative games and activities is that they can be varied according to the ages and talents of the participants; they can be adapted to every learning situation. Vary the games to fit the profile of the participants.

Age is a factor for each game. Please do not take age guidelines literally; experiment, and enjoy as you go along.

But it is important to consider age, and at a deeper level, the growth stage of the children.

A thorough and meaningful understanding of the growth stages of children is one of the best tools for all education. Success with these games depends in large measure on your understanding of child development. With this understanding, games can be chosen and applied with an efficacy that is astounding. (Toward that aim, we have included an Appendix with information about Natural Learning Relationships in this third edition.)

The attitude of the game leader is critical. Children are naturally attuned to accept guidance from elders and so are able to read us in disarmingly straightforward ways. If the leader does not genuinely wish for cooperation, or in any way exhibits prejudice or manipulation, the playing of cooperative games becomes hypocritical. *As you model, so you teach.*

If a game does not work well the first time, come back to it later. Sometimes it takes several attempts before children grasp the sense of a game. Cooperative games and activities are not woven into the fabric of most of North American play. Children have not been watching cooperative games on TV since they were born. Therefore, go slowly. Do not attempt too many variations immediately. That creates the image of desperation. It is better to try lots of different games. Be honest; be patient; and enlist the children's help. You might be surprised how much children are honored by such a request and rise to the occasion with cooperative ideas.

If a child does not want to play, do not force her. Do not allow her to disrupt the group, either. Our experience has been that, after observing, most children either join or find a different constructive activity. There is something about the cooperative nature of the event that increases a child's safe space. The atmosphere becomes gentler, and the children sense it.

Go ahead and play. Read through the games once or twice; familiarize yourself with the ones you are to play that day; and then go for it. Why not? You've got nothing to lose. Your ability to facilitate will come from experience and will come rather quickly.

Bring your sense of humor. This is the most important point of all. Make jokes, even silly ones. Lighten up; play games; and let everyone enjoy themselves. Humor is the most healthy environment for everyone — and one in which you will have access to the most information concerning the children.

Games in Different Situations

Cooperative games and activities have been used successfully in all learning environments, at parties, within the immediate family and the extended family, and at large group gatherings. We have played them with whole communities, camps, public and private schools, people who are disabled, and homeschooling collectives. They provide an excellent focus that allows appreciation of everyone's abilities in a friendly, comfortable way. Self-esteem grows; the inner sense of peace and interconnectedness comes alive.

There are games that serve as icebreakers, as a medium for feelings, as concentration intensifiers, as artistic and thinking enhancers, and as group and individual centering techniques. With a minimum of effort and a maximum of fun, cooperative games provide a way to recognize and integrate the rhythms of the participants.

In the experience described at the beginning of this introduction, the situation was conflict within a large school group. We would like to close with descriptions of two more experiences, each of a very different nature. These three examples hardly exhaust all the situations amenable to the use of cooperative games. Hopefully, taken together, they will stimulate you to find your own approach to using them. If you require more information, feel free to write to us. We are available for consultations to help you create an application suitable for your situation.

Early in our career, we had the honor of guiding a group of children on a nature walk every Friday. There were about a dozen in the class, ranging in age from 6 to 12. Our rhythm was to take an hour-long walk in the forest that surrounds our community, have a snack, and then play cooperative games. We had lunch and then it was more games, storytelling, or acting. The aim of the class was for the children to learn how to be friends. This aim they knew. When conflict arose we stopped our activity and worked toward a resolution. No cliques were ever allowed. We all agreed that being friends is not all that easy. Every one of them was glad for the opportunity to learn. They are also angry that this skill is not usually taught, for they clearly perceive the trouble grownups have relating.

Surprisingly, nature was not the primary attraction for the children. That honor belonged to cooperative games and activities and the social dynamic arising from them. When we came across a red-tailed hawk doing a mating flight, examined coyote scat to determine its diet, surprised a flock of wild turkeys, or collected wildflowers to press, there was always great delight, wonder, and appreciation of nature. But these were not sought. The children preferred to play cooperative games. This, to us, was something of a shock but a tribute to the power of these games in satisfying a genuine need of the children.

Their favorite game is not listed in this book. They created it themselves and, to be honest, we do not know all the rules. It is called "Wild Horses," and it has something to do with playacting horses, mountain lions, people, sheep, and whatever or whomever any participant wants to be. This game evolved from a game they invented about the Greek myths. All we asked was that everyone be included, that there be no real violence, and that no cliques formed. At first there was some resistance to these guidelines, but soon we didn't even need to mention them. Every now and then we checked in with different children to make sure they were included in a satisfactory way. We were never disappointed.

The children's created game, "Wild Horses," did not appear until the class had been together over a year. We had gone through many games, most of them with success. Most games had their moment of being preferred, but on the whole each has had a similar amount of consideration. Often the children came up with their own variations.

One last experience concerns a mother and her six-year-old boy. We were asked to help when the mother was concluding a painful and violent divorce from the boy's father. The boy — bright, energetic, and sensitive — was having a difficult time in school. He was strong and liked the spotlight. His classmates had seized upon this to use him to personify their own negative tendencies. As a result, he was often dared and taunted. Like his father, he responded violently. The label of "bad" was hung on him, and any time the others needed to participate in "badness," this boy was the chosen object.

And, to be sure, part of him liked it. It was attention and power, and even those who did not like him needed him. One boy, frail in body and underdeveloped emotionally, particularly enjoyed leaning on him, getting hit, and both of them being punished.

While work with this family proceeded on many levels, one small but important part involved cooperative games. We wanted to reawaken this boy's sense of belonging and rightful place in the world. If he could feel that he belonged on this planet and in his family, then his life would be of value, and destructive behaviors would diminish.

Two cooperative games were chosen, and both worked very well. First, to give the mother the information of the disposition of the boy each day, an animal game was introduced around the breakfast table. The mother had many pictures of animals — everything from rearing cobras to cuddling koalas. Each morning she would hold one up, and each person would say how they resembled that animal that day. There was a younger sister in the house, and the three of them would play together. Often they acted out their animal feelings. Of course, their moods became family knowledge, and that instantly released some tension. And the mother had a much clearer picture of how to apply other remedies we were using in our attempt to improve the overall situation.

The other game was a morning family stretch game. Like the one above, it was very simple. Everyone met by the fireplace for a five-minute stretch together, with each family member being the leader on a rotating basis. They soon added the variation of a hand-coordination game. They now started their day taking a relaxed breath together. The connection that the boy needed to experience was present. He responded favorably, and his good health and well-being were soon restored.

Friends, thank you for giving us the opportunity to write about cooperative games and activities. We truly hope you will experiment with them and find them as useful as we have. In this critical juncture of human evolution, they can help teach cooperation, respect, and friendship. These are qualities that go a long way and of which we can never get enough.

If we can be of any help to you, please do not hesitate to write.

Peace,

Josette Luvmour, PhD
Ba Luvmour, MA
www.luvmourconsulting.com

Preface to the Third Edition

*E*VERYONE WANTS TO CREATE A GOOD AND JUST SOCIETY that cares for the education of children. Educational choices reflect values. Engaging in cooperative activities with children as part of their education offers a playful way to grow together that benefits everyone involved.

Children are always changing. When we create rich, developmentally appropriate, and playfully engaging environments for children, we are shaping and creating a healthier and more socially just future. In cooperative games, there are no winners or losers. When playing cooperatively, there is no dominant power person. Rather, helping one another is the way we all succeed. These cooperative games are structured so that players must use pro-social skills such as sharing, encouraging, listening, and participating in order for everyone to succeed together.

We are delighted to have the honor to present this third edition of *Everyone Wins* at the request of New Society Publishers. Perhaps you can imagine how full of excitement we are to learn that the *Everyone Wins* games book has traveled in the pockets of more than 25,000 school teachers, youth group leaders, camp counselors, kindergarten teachers, playground monitors, outdoor education teachers, and many others since it was first published in

1990. Inspired by the receptivity and usefulness of the first edition, we have added 12 new games that we have been playing for the past 20 years.

As you read through this introduction you will learn about our experiences with cooperative games and activities throughout our 30-plus years of use. We ground games in child development and introduce you to how cooperative play is a foundation to building resilience. We also discuss the importance of play, learning by doing, and meeting the needs of today's children to build a more positive social world. In addition, we introduce you to how to use cooperative activities to learn about children, observe obstacles to healthy relationships, and apply remedies. Moreover we discuss the hidden benefits to adults who play. Explore with us as we share with you how everyone grows together while engaging cooperative activities with the children in your lives.

Our experiences with cooperative play

Since its first publication more than 28 years ago, *Everyone Wins* has had a profound impact on an incredibly diverse group of readers and their practices. Specifically, as reported by teachers, camp counselors, family coaches, and youth group leaders, these games, activities, and initiatives have had great value in assessing interpersonal dynamics, teaching social justice, and assessing developmental capacities.

We have used games, cooperative activities, and methods like these in schools of every pedagogical type, in board rooms to build common vision, at conferences to build community, in classrooms for interpersonal learning and to increase friendship, in schools to inspire a culture of meaning, and with adults and children in all walks of life.

In addition, the book has been used by child psychologists and family therapists. It has been sold in many countries, is included in the national data bank on conflict resolution, and has won the Parent's Choice Award. We never would have guessed that this little book that began on scraps of paper would have such incredible impact on so many great people.

Everyone growing together

We have honed cooperative games and activities over the years by playing with others and paying attention while we do it. In all honesty, we have grown as much as the many participants in the process. In our experience, there are few engagements that have such a major impact on the future of humanity as conscientiously connecting to each child as we play. We are shaping the future by our presence, genuine participation, full engagement, and enthusiasm to meet children where they are. We are truly the child's context and part of their environment. Who we are is what we teach. Engaging in self-reflection and questioning who we are as we play offers us unparalleled opportunity for growth.

Grounding games in whole-child development

Natural Learning Relationships (NLR) is a practical and applicable whole-child developmental science. NLR details the psychological, emotional, physical, and spiritual components of optimal well-being. Furthermore, it describes the dynamics by which these capacities emerge within each stage of childhood. Relationship based, NLR includes the context of the child's life: family, school, and background. It is founded on both fieldwork and the literature in child development, family systems, and contiguous psychological disciplines.

We are all born with innate capacities that need relationship in order to come out and be actualized. When we play with children and nurture their developmental needs, we are recognizing, strengthening, and nurturing a quality that was there from the outset.

With knowledge of Natural Learning Relationships whole-child development, adults have (1) increased competence with children, (2) better communication on the child's developmental level, (3) fewer conflicts and more understanding for the child's age-specific capabilities, (4) improved relationships with each child, and (5) less frustration.

Life stages contain capacities, but development occurs *in relationship*. Developmental needs are provided during play because development is emergent (ever changing). Simply, this means that our kind awareness of the child's internal state is a statement of acceptance — obvious, subtle, explicit, tacit, or implied. When a child comes into this warm environment he opens up; imagination can flourish, and the child develops the ability to feel resourceful, bounce back from small set-backs, be a creative problem solver, ask for help when needed, and thrive in well-being. Details about Natural Learning Relationships can be found in Appendix A.

Knowing the characteristics of developmental stages gives the adult insights into the child's needs, the different perceptions of each age, and the best environment to support well-being.

Knowledge of child development is important during play because when we know how children develop and grow, we know how each age child organizes her world. We can see through the child's eyes and apprehend who she is. That knowledge leads to better connection with the child, guides healthier decisions, and inspires more appropriate expectations. As expectations become relational to the child's developmental markers, frustration decreases for both adult and child. Children are happier when their developmental needs are met. Better connection with a child means that trust develops between adult and child. Trust leads to internal experience of well-being.

Brain development and play

> What the social sciences and affective neurosciences are revealing is that the legacy of our intelligent brain is our social mind.
>
> (Immordino-Yang, 2016)

Relationships in life shape the structural development of the brain. Our minds are open to ways in which interpersonal experiences continue to facilitate development throughout our lifespan.

The brain is a complex emergent system. The behavior of the whole cannot be predicted from the parts, because the combinations of all parts are nonlinear (often unpredictable), emergent (ever changing), self-organizing, and adaptive.

Experience shapes the brain. The brain changes throughout our lives, from the moment we are born until the moment we die. Moreover, our brains require stimulation and connection to survive and thrive. Close supportive relationships that nurture our developmental needs will stimulate positive access to our innate capacities and optimal well-being.

In addition, the field of neuroscience has revealed that emotion and learning are inextricably interconnected and interdependent. Yes, cognition and emotion cannot be separated. What is more, we tend to think deeply about things we feel for and care about. Making meaningful decisions without emotion is neurobiologically impossible (Immordino-Yang, 2016). While engaging in play and cooperative activities, we develop emotions that guide our social endeavors; promote exploration; and lead us to discover empathy, care, compassion, and interest in others and in life.

Brain development occurs in relationship. We posit that cooperative games and activities lead to emotional intelligence. One aim of this book is to give you the tools and information so that you can make those relationships support the optimal well-being of the child and in so doing nurture your own growth and development.

Observation, obstacles, and remedies

Knowledge about child development gives us the tools to observe children at play and use cooperative games to identify obstacles and apply remedies to build trust, improve friendships, and increase intimacy. Creating classroom culture with the use of cooperative activities is a tool at your fingertips.

As you observe, you will find that children organize their world differently in each stage of their development. As children grow, the different organization of their world influences the way relationship is engaged. Observation of behaviors, vocabulary used, how children play, what they do with their body, and more gives us information about their internal world. To enter their world and form successful relationships requires understanding of each child's moment.

When children are in the company of someone who genuinely cares, they feel supported to be who they are. Learning how to focus on children's strengths while also caring for their developmental needs sets up a safe environment in which children experience trust. Providing emotional nurturing by being trustworthy adults creates an environment of trustworthiness in which children can relax, open up, and be themselves as they play. Such an environment is a turning point for children as difficulties melt away. Knowledge about child development is critical to understanding developmentally appropriate ways to provide play environments of security, safety, trust, and authenticity.

As a result of staying connected with children in this way, we grow in confidence and inner-resilience. One facilitator said, "I remember what I need to do right now in this moment to help this child. I know I am doing the right thing. I just keep picking up and going on. I have stamina; I stay with it." The first things she asks herself are, "What age is this child? What was the trigger? What does this child really need?" There are always insights when we are able to see children as they are, in the moment. "I find that it's easier for me to be compassionate with myself, with the children, and with other adults when I question what a child really needs."

Facilitator neutrality

No teacher or facilitator is ever fully objective. We are all conditioned by our life experiences. Consequently, it is very important that we each take a second look and question how our life experiences have affected our values, beliefs, and judgments. As facilitators, we must check to see to what extent our position of power in the group affects our relationships and shapes our views of the children. Do we encourage all participants to develop along their own unique paths? To what extent might our educational history "domesticate" children to fit obediently into the roles required of them by the dominant culture? To what extent can we liberate children to be critical, creative, free, active, and responsible decision makers? Can we find a way to present a core problem back to the group for them to search for solutions? Can we offer our input as a starting point for further discussion and not as the formal "truth" or the definitive answer?

Our role as the facilitator throughout cooperative activities is not to give answers but to set up a process through which the group can look for their own answers and explore their ideas and systems of thinking.

The importance of play

We learn as we play. Play is an activity done for its own sake, characterized by means rather than an end. In cooperative play, the process is more important than the end point or goal. There is no success or failure in play, no mandatory achievement. Thus, a primary aspect of play is safety and freedom. *Play is the medium of learning for all age children — even for adults.*

The more you know about child development, the more competent and the better able you will be to create environments and relationships that give children optimal access to innate capacities at every stage of their growth. An example is how children play at learning rules through the medium of the game:

- BodyBeing children (ages 0 through 7) play with words, develop language, and actualize a more complex self.... Play remains the medium in which mastery develops.
- FeelingBeing children (ages 8 through 12) play with social relationships.
- IdealBeing children (ages 13 through 17) idealize a self and play with identities.
- ReasonableBeing children (ages 18 through 23) — organizing their world to optimize interconnectedness — play with system creation. Play leads to language, but then language becomes the field of play. Moreover, language

cannot be restricted to words or verbal-linguistic intelligence. (Luvmour, 2006)

Less play and more mandated learning results in increased anxiety and depression, delayed emotional and social development, inhibited executive functioning skills, and diminished intellectual vitality.

Play is a fundamental component of learning and allows all people (young children, adolescents, and adults) to engage in the deepest and most meaningful forms of learning, maximizing their creativity, and igniting intellectual passion.

Learning by doing

Play is what children do. Playing is learning. Playing with children is one of the most important activities we do with them, because play involves social, emotional, and cognitive development. Playful activities promote connection with others, problem solving, and social-skills development, and they provide a medium to work through stress and emotional tension and to have fun. During play, children grow to understand boundaries and limits — while at the same time pushing limits to explore what might happen (a very healthy thing to do).

Social and emotional learning is supported in cooperative play. According to Maurice Elias, director of Rutgers University's Social and Emotional Learning Lab, social emotional learning is the process through which we learn to recognize and manage emotions, care about others, make good decisions, behave ethically and responsibly, and avoid negative behaviors. Children's social, emotional, and character development is promoted during cooperative activities. Above all, we should never lose sight of the importance of our modeling the value of close relationships, supporting and caring for one another, and enjoyment.

Building our social world

Discovering that cooperative games impact our society for the better is an understatement. Through cooperative play children increase their language skills, develop self-trust, negotiate skills, hypothesize, and empathize with others; these are all building blocks that are fundamental to life-long success in the workplace, in marriage, and in every community.

Relationships impact learning. Cooperative activities and games are always relational and emergent. In this context, relational means opportunities for personal and authentic encounters in which the child is known and feels that his feelings are understood. Emergent refers to the state of being in continual process, never arriving (no end state), and always moving and changing. Emergent systems continually interact with the environment — changing and adapting. Interactions in groups of human beings left free to regulate themselves tend toward spontaneous order. Our relationship with children during play requires us to adapt the game as we go, no matter how well planned or organized a game may be. A beauty of these games is that you can be creative and adapt them to meet the needs of the children and environment you are in. Many times children will come up with their own adaptations that improve everyone's experience. When we surrender to these spontaneous and creative adaptations, we are transformed in the process.

Children need meaningful experiences that connect new information with what they already know to be true. This forms "webs" of information that relates and is grouped into sets and subsets. With this information children construct their understanding of the world, adding from their experiences and observations to their repertoire of learning. When we see ourselves as part of the play environment, we can move with it and influence what happens, but we cannot control it. Through continuous facilitated interactions and interplay, children experience their contributions as meaningful and valuable. This allows children to be active agents in shaping their world and thereby creating meaning.

Children who experience themselves as *socially valuable* throughout their childhood feel trust for themselves and for others. Trusting children have the greatest likelihood of facilitating the transition to a socially just world. When each child's contributions are recognized, appreciated, supported, and engaged, participation in social justice becomes a societal norm.

Our job is to simply know the children we are with and meet children where they are to build relationship. The games presented in this book offer you relationship-based activities for all ages to build your social world toward meaningful, connected, and socially just relationships.

Meeting the needs in today's world

The news is filled with sad stories about violence in schools. We need to create an effective response now that promotes a sense of connection and personal well-being while also advancing resilience with a sense of purpose. Prevention means being proactive.

Supportive relationships and positive learning experiences are keys to student well-being, learning, and success. Needed is an approach that values the human spirit and the development of the child as a whole. Children need to be supported in emotional well-being and other non-academic facets of the whole child that underpin their reaching their highest potential and promote positive attributes as well as meaning in life.

Within the family children develop the values and emotional metabolism they will take into the world to sustain their way of living. Within each family children are learning ethical and moral standards through role models. We are the models that children shape their relationships after and discover how to care for one another in mutually supportive and caring ways.

When children are in the company of someone who genuinely cares, they feel supported to become imaginative and resilient. Feelings of connection and a willingness to collaborate are the result. Experiential learning that occurs in cooperative activities builds connection, strengthens emotional bonds, and promotes resilience. These activities give you the tools to improve social and emotional well-being wherever you are with children (e.g., in school, playgroups, family gatherings, independent learning, and home-based education). Restoring relationships through games is an amazingly effective response to the needs in today's world. We are creating and shaping the social world in which we live during play.

Cooperative play as a foundation to building resilience

Mental health is more than an absence of pathology. Resilience is the ability to bounce back in the face of significant life challenges or adversity and thrive despite negative life experiences. It is more than coping (which can be seen as a protective factor of managing stressful circumstances); resilience has to do with recovering and overcoming adversity to actualize a positive outcome.

Empathy, compassion, and cooperation have played a fundamental role in how we evolved as a cooperative species. Empathy learned during play also expands our world, helping us to feel or imagine the feelings of another. The result is empathy that motivates us to care about each other and act with kindness. In a world of indifference, isolation, loneliness, and destructive trends (even in children), activities that promote cooperation and social learning are needed now more than ever.

Educators who nurture the development of trust, care, and empathy serve as role models that can promote self-control and resilience — especially when educators are backed up by parental support in the home. Our experience and research has shown that adults benefit as much as children when we care for and nurture the development of resilience in our children and students.

Hidden benefits to adults who play

> We do not stop playing because we grow old.... We grow old because we stop playing.
>
> (George Bernard Shaw, playwright)

Playing with children is a process that doesn't only make us more mindful, compassionate, and resilient but deeply transforms us and the way we live our lives. Everyone who teaches learns.

> Parenting is a field of play in which uncertainty, ambiguity, and adaptation are ongoing parts of our lives. There is a tremendous amount of helplessness and uncertainty. At the same time, our parenting can inspire us to live authentically, to be more aware, to gain self-knowledge, and to grow in ways that were once unimaginable.
>
> (Luvmour, 2017)

Every day is a new opportunity to connect with our children, develop their strengths, and help them to access meaning and purpose. Meeting children where they are with an attitude of acceptance and playfulness is a service that is simultaneously beneficial to our hearts. We are continually humbled by the enormous opportunity that meeting a child's developmental moment offers us to grow. The wonderful news is that we get many opportunities — it's not once and done. To engage with children this way requires our willing attention and active presence. These ideas will be easier to understand when they are seen, felt, and experienced in the context of play.

Remembering that we have an inexorable tendency toward wholeness, toward goodness, we are ever reorganizing in relationship with the children in our lives. Ba and I feel great gratitude for anyone who appreciates the opportunity to grow together with the children in your lives.

Who we are is what we teach.

This book is for

- Children everywhere
- Teachers of every age group
- Home-education communities
- Teachers of interpersonal curriculum in education
- All professionals who promote emotional skills
- Parents
- Counselors and therapists who work with children and families
- Childcare professionals (and anyone who cares for children)
- Youth leaders
- Camp counselors
- Grandparents
- All playful relatives and friends

- Therapists, marriage and family counselors, and health professionals
- Anyone with a child in their life

Special note

Pronouns are alternated throughout this book. *He, she,* and *they* are used interchangeably and do not indicate preference for one over the other by the authors.

Invitation

We close this brief introduction with an invitation. We invite everyone reading this — parents, students, teachers (of any kind), and anyone who is interested in working for a better future — to engage in play with children of all ages. Please use the materials offered in this book as well as develop your own variations. Be creative. Above all else, enjoy yourself and enjoy the children

> *Josette Luvmour, PhD, and Ba Luvmour, MA*
> **For information**
> **web: www.luvmourconsulting.com**
> em: josette@luvmourconsulting.com
> em: ba@luvmourconsulting.com
> Podcasts: Meetings with Remarkable Educators

- available at Google Play, iTunes, www.remarkable-educators.com/podcast, and wherever you get your podcasts

References:

Elias, Maurice, J. Rutgers Social and Emotional Learning Laboratory.

Immordino-Yang, M. H. (2016). *Emotions, Learning, and the Brain: Exploring the Educational Implications of Affective Neuroscience.* New York: Norton.

Luvmour, B. (2006). *Optimal Parenting: Using Natural Learning Rhythms to Nurture the Whole Child.* Boulder, CO: Sentient.

Luvmour, J. (2017). *Grow Together: Parenting as A path to Well-Being, Wisdom, and Joy.* North Charleston, SC: Create Space Publishing.

How to Use This Book

UNDER THE NAME OF EACH GAME you will find four categories containing information to help you evaluate its usefulness in different situations. These categories are:

Activity Level

"1" is the most active and "5" is the least active. The games are arranged by activity level. You will find the activities listed in order from 1 to 5.

Age

Age refers to the minimum age a participant needs to be to enjoy the game. All games are indexed by age at the back of the book.

Location

"In" means the game is best played indoors. "Out" means it must be played outdoors. "Inside or Outside" means the game can be played indoors or outdoors.

Group Size

This refers to the minimum amount of players necessary to play the game. All games are indexed by group size at the back of the book.

How to Use the Indices

Games within an index are in alphabetical order. Thus if you want to find a game that needs six players, go to the Games Group Size Index and look up "Six or More Players." The games are alphabetically listed. If your players are seven and eight years old, then go to the Games Age Level Index, look up the age and cross reference with those games selected from the Games Group Size index. You are now ready to play.

The body of the game information consists of the *Description*, *Variations*, and *Special Hints*. If *Materials* are needed, they are indicated in this section as well. Don't be afraid to try your own variations — and please drop us a line with any new hints you may discover in your play!

Activity Level 1

Elbow Tag

Activity Level: 1   **Age Level: 8+**
Location: Inside or outside   **Group Size: 10+**
Materials: Sturdy shoes

Game Description:

Designate an "It" and a "Rabbit."

Arrange all other players in a circle in pairs. Between each pair create a space of (at least) a full extended arm's length. The members of each pair hook elbows with one another then extend the other elbow, hook style, out from the side with hand on hip.

The players who are It and Rabbit start opposite one another on the outside of the circle.

On the "Go!" command, It tries to tag Rabbit. They can run inside or outside the circle (but not far). It's a good idea to define boundaries. Rabbit runs to avoid being tagged and can hook into any free elbow. The person next to the hooked person then unhooks with his partner and becomes the Rabbit.

If Rabbit is tagged, they immediately switch places, and the Rabbit becomes It and turns to chase the new Rabbit. The new Rabbit must hook up elbows with any player in the circle quickly. Hooking and unhooking happens often.

Special Hints:

Remind players, often if necessary, to hook up quickly. Facilitate everyone getting a turn, and try to not let a fast runner dominate the game by staying Rabbit for too long.

Chase in the Ocean

Activity Level: 1
Location: Inside or outside

Age Level: 4+
Group Size: 6

Game Description:

A caller shouts "ship": and all the children run to the base at which she points. After counting three, the caller chases with arms outspread ready to gobble any child not on the base and touching another. The caller — if older — usually just misses.

Variations:

Sardine: All the children must be on base and touching one another.

Crab: The children must be back to back with one another.

Special Hints:

Make three or four areas to run to so caller can surprise the children by pointing as she calls.

Smaug's Jewels

Activity Level: 1
Location: Inside or outside
Materials: A rag

Age Level: 4+
Group Size: 5

Game Description:

The "treasure" — a rag — is placed on the ground. One child guards it. All the others try to grab it. If a thief is touched by the guardian of the treasure she takes three steps back.

Variations:

Play with two guardians and have the tagged thief take five steps back.

Special Hints:

Be the referee.

Dho – Dho – Dho

Activity Level: 1   **Age Level: 7+**
Location: Inside or outside   **Group Size: 8**

Game Description:
Two teams face off. While holding her breath, one player from a team crosses the line and tries to tag one or more players and make it back to her side; all the time holding her breath and with enough air left to say Dho-Dho-Dho. All tagged players switch teams. If the player does not succeed she joins the other team.

Variations:
Vary playing area size.

Special Hints:
Not fully cooperative so monitor closely. Valuable for energetic ones to let off steam.

Giants-Wizards-Elves

Activity Level: 1   **Age Level: 5+**
Location: Inside or outside   **Group Size: 8**

Game Description:
Two teams. Each team agrees on a posture for a giant, a wizard, and an elf and shows it to the other team. Each huddles and decides which creature it will be. Teams come to center line and at the count of three make the chosen posture and say the creature's name. Wizards fool Giants. Giants beat Elves. Elves trick wizards. Whoever loses has to beat it back to their safety about 20 feet away from the center line before the other team catches them. Those caught switch teams.

Special Hints:
Similar to Rock-Paper-Scissors with action.

On Your Knees

Activity Level: 1   **Age Level: 7+**
Location: Inside or outside   **Group Size: 1**

Game Description:
Kneel down with back straight. Lift heels towards rump and grab ankles. Take knee steps as you are now balanced on your kneecaps.

Variations:
Try it as a group — grabbing a partner's ankle in a relay race or a dance.

Special Hints:
Make sure no knees get hurt.

Emotional Relay Race

Activity Level: 1   **Age Level: 9+**
Location: Inside or outside   **Group Size: 12**
Materials: Three bowls and three pieces of fruit

Game Description:
Three teams — each lined up behind the piece of fruit of its choice. Each player takes time to come up with their sound and movement for "sad," "angry," and "happy." The bowls are set distance away. Each player picks up the fruit — runs to the bowl — puts it down — does "angry" three times — runs back to the start — does "happy" twice — back to fruit for "sad" twice — brings the fruit back to the start — takes a bite — and on to the next player.

Variations:
Can substitute other emotions or do it in tandem.

Special Hints:
Players should be in a playful mood right from the start.

Hop As One

Activity Level: 1	**Age Level: 5+**
Location: Inside or outside	**Group Size: 5**

Game Description:
Players in a line — except for the leader — lift and extend left leg so the person behind can grab ankle or heel. They then place right hand on right shoulder of person in front for support. Now it's hop time.

Variations:
Switch sides — do a dance — collective timing — over obstacles.

Special Hints:
Remind them of careful coordination. Practice before getting discouraged.

Blanket Volleyball

Activity Level: 1	**Age Level: 8+**
Location: Outside	**Group Size: 6**
Materials: Blankets and balls

Game Description:
Players hold the edge of the blanket. They place a ball on the blanket. They then toss the ball up by cooperatively manipulating the blanket. They try to catch it in the middle of the blanket. Score is cumulative.

Variations:
Use volleyball or beach ball. Change blanket size; define boundaries; use net. Pass the ball between two groups with blankets.

Special Hints:
Switch positions on blanket; make sure little ones do not get hurt. Skill needed. Greatly helps energetic ones to center on cooperation.

Upside Down Cycling

Activity Level: 1   **Age Level: 4+**
Location: Inside or outside   **Group Size: 2**

Game Description:
Lie on back and touch bottom of feet with bottom of partner's feet. Do simultaneous cycling action first in one direction then in another.

Variations:
Try three players; eyes closed; use music.

Special Hints:
Works well for all shapes and sizes of people — even those in conflict.

Dragon Dodge Ball

Activity Level: 1   **Age Level: 5+**
Location: Outside   **Group Size: 7+**
Materials: Sponge balls or rubber balls

Game Description:
All join hands in a large circle. Two people form a Dragon. One, the head, stands upright. The other, the tail, holds the head's hips and sticks her fanny out. The others pass balls around and try to hit the Dragon's fanny. If a ball hits the ground it must be passed before being thrown at the Dragon. No player can hold a ball more than three seconds. Passer who sets up the hit becomes the new tail. The former tail becomes the head. Use at least two balls at a time.

Variations:
More dragons. Vary circle size.

Special Hints:
Warn against collisions. Excellent for working out aggression.

How Do You Do?

Activity Level: 1 **Age Level: 8+**
Location: Outside **Group Size: 10**

Game Description:

All but two players join hands and form a circle. The outside two are a lost ship looking for port. They choose a pair from the circle. Holding hands, the chosen pair and the outside pair run around the circle in opposite directions attempting to get back to the vacant spot. As they pass one another, they must stop, shake hands and say "How do you do?" before continuing.

Variations:

Hop or skip around the circle. Travel with eyes closed and runners touching the circle as they move.

Special Hints:

Explain rules and direction of travel carefully. Warn against crashes. Make sure all get a turn.

Up and Around

Activity Level: 1 **Age Level: 8+**
Location: Outside **Group Size: 2**
Materials: Two-foot stick; belts; string; rubber ball

Game Description:

With a string tied to a broomstick, hang a tennis ball just above the ground. Children support the stick at their waists against their belts. Without using their hands they try to swing the ball over the stick.

Variations:

Make it wind and unwind. Play with eyes closed.

Special Hints:

Let little ones use their hands.

Blow the Ball

Activity Level: 1   **Age Level: 4+**
Location: Inside   **Group Size: 5**
Materials: Ping pong ball and mats or blankets

Game Description:
One child lies on stomach on a mat. Six others grab edges of the mat and pull while the child blows the ping pong ball across the room. How fast can they do it?

Variations:
As a relay race with or without obstacles.

Special Hints:
Make sure no one player is overburdened.

Go Tag

Activity Level: 1   **Age Level: 8+**
Location: Outside   **Group Size: 10**

Game Description:
Everyone squats in a line. Alternate players facing opposite directions, to the right and left. Everyone but person in front — *the chaser* — or back — *the chased* — kneels. The chaser can tap a squatter who then takes up the chase. The first chaser takes the squatter's position. The chaser must always go in the same direction. The chased can go in either direction. For example: Players 1–10 line up. Players 1, 3, 5, 7, 9 face to the right. Players 2, 4, 6, 8, 10 face to the left. Player 1 chases 10. If 1 decides that 7 has a better chance to tag 10, she taps 7 and takes her place. Player 7 takes up the chase. It's a game of timing and cunning.

Special Hints:
Practice a few times so all understand. Give everyone a chance to do everything.

It

Activity Level: 1
Location: Outside

Age Level: 6+
Group Size: 16

Game Description:

Two teams. Each goes to a different tree, leaving about 150 feet between them. One player calls It and starts running toward the other tree. If she touches the tree she scores a point. But anyone who touches her or is touched by her automatically becomes It. She can deliberately touch another on her team, who then continues toward the same goal. But if touched by a member of the other team, It is transferred and that player tries to move to her tree. No one can block or help the runner as she advances toward her tree.

Special Hints:

It is as if a spirit is being transferred at touch. Points are hard to score but not impossible.

Cooperative Relay Races

Activity Level: 1
Location: Outside

Age Level: 5+
Group Size: 8+

Materials: Varies according to type of race

Game Description:

Divide children into teams. They race for a best collective time while negotiating a course.

Variations:

Obstacles; crawling; running backwards; skipping; with golf ball in a spoon.

Special Hints:

Let children make up their own order of running; be prepared for it to get crazy.

True or False

Activity Level: 1   **Age Level: 7+**
Location: Outside   **Group Size: 8**

Game Description:
Two teams, "Trues" and "Falses," face off in the middle of a field with a safety area for each team about 20 feet behind. Leader makes a statement about nature. If correct, Trues chase Falses. If incorrect, Falses chase Trues. Anyone caught goes to the other team.

Variations:
Statements about academics; or any other subject.

Special Hints:
Let confusion reign before supplying the correct answer. Choose questions appropriate to knowledge of players. This is an excellent teaching game.

Big Toe

Activity Level: 1   **Age Level: 7+**
Location: Inside or outside   **Group Size: 1**

Game Description:
Squat down, grab your toes, bend your knees and try to jump forward as far as possible.

Variations:
Do it as a collective long jump or choreograph as a dance.

Special Hints:
You'll improve with practice. It is funny as a group.

Pull Together

Activity Level: 1
Location: Outside
Materials: Large strong rope

Age Level: 5+
Group Size: 10

Game Description:
Leader divides children into two equal teams so when they pull on the rope as hard as they can, neither team moves.

Variations:
Tie a rope around a heavy object and try to move it.

Toby Terrific Turtle

Activity Level: 1
Location: Outside
Materials: Obstacles; green clothes; old blanket

Age Level: 6+
Group Size: 5

Game Description:
Group huddles under blanket. All are blindfolded except the leader. Group moves together through obstacles as quickly as possible. Everyone gets a chance to be leader.

Variations:
Play in mud puddles! Group can hold hands.

Special Hints:
Be careful!

Catch the Dragon's Tail

Activity Level: 1   **Age Level: 7+**
Location: Outside   **Group Size: 8**
Materials: Handkerchief

Game Description:
Players line up with arms around the waist of the person in front. Last one has a handkerchief in her pocket. The player at the head of the line tries to grab the handkerchief. No part of the Dragon may break.

Variations:
Two Dragons attempt to catch each other's tails. Rotate the players.

Hug Tag

Activity Level: 1   **Age Level: 4+**
Location: Outside   **Group Size: 8**
Materials: Strips of cloth and hats or easily held objects

Game Description:
About one-sixth of the group are given strips of cloth. They are "It" and can tag any other player. The others are safe only when hugging another player. If two or more players keep hugging, "It" can take three steps backwards and say "1-2-3 Break!" Those players have to find new players to hug.

Special Hints:
Pick boundaries carefully. Keep the game moving. Great fun for everyone. Equalizes varied talents.

Obstacle Course

Activity Level: 1   **Age Level: 3+**
Location: Outside   **Group Size: 5**
Materials: Anything and everything

Game Description:
Children design their own obstacle course and run it.

Variations:
Infinite.

Special Hints:
Make sure all who want to participate have a chance to do so.

Creative Monkey Bars

Activity Level: 1   **Age Level: 6+**
Location: Outside   **Group Size: 3**
Materials: PVC pipe and fittings

Game Description:
Using PVC pipe and fittings, children design and construct and play on their own monkey bars.

Variations:
Make their own furniture.

Special Hints:
Materials can be expensive, but self-esteem is worth it! Switch children around so that balance is achieved. When they get the idea, encourage them to switch themselves.

Couples Sports

Activity Level: 1   **Age Level: 8+**
Location: Outside   **Group Size: 10**
Materials: Balls and leg ties

Game Description:
Play baseball with legs tied together or holding hands.

Variations:
Any ball game or tag.

Special Hints:
Match pairs with attention to athletic ability. Use small playing space.

Activity Level 2

Between You and Me

Activity Level: 2 **Age Level: 9+**
Location: Inside **Group Size: 8+**

Game Description:

Gather all players. Define the boundaries of this game and make sure all players know to stay inside the boundaries as they move around.

Each player must pick a guardian (in their mind), but they do not tell anyone who it is. Then, again only to themselves, each player picks an antagonist (in their mind). Only the players know their own choices.

The facilitator then says "Go," and everyone must try to keep their guardian between themselves and their antagonist.

Variations:

Feel free to make up variations in relationship to your group.

Special Hints:

Make sure players do not talk or give away their choices.

Make sure boundaries provide space to maneuver but not too much space; distance dilutes the game.

Ask the players, "Who can tell me what a 'guardian' is?"

Ask the players, "Who can tell me what an 'antagonist' is?"

Go with the best definitions or add to the explanations given.

Upset Fruit Basket

Activity Level: 2   **Age Level: 5+**
Location: Inside or outside   **Group Size: 9+**
Materials: Chairs

Game Description:

Make small groups of three persons.

Name each group as a fruit (e.g., "bananas," "pears," "apples"). Place a circle of chairs, with one less than the total amount of people playing.

Everyone sits in a chair except one player. The person not sitting in a chair calls out one of the fruit names. Everyone in that group (only) must switch chairs. The caller also attempts to occupy one of the chairs. So you have four people vying for three chairs. The player left standing calls out the next fruit. If the player says "Upset fruit basket," then everyone must switch.

Variations:

Use pillows on the floor, carpet squares, or designated spots on a gym mat instead of chairs.

Have the players take a break between each round.

Special Hints:

Be careful that overzealous players don't crash into one another. Don't allow the player calling out the fruit to take too long to call out the next fruit. Adults and children can play together.

I've Been Tagged

Activity Level: 2   **Age Level: 8+**
Location: Inside or outside   **Group Size: 10+**
Materials: Rope or boundary marker that lies flat on the floor

Game Description:

Define a circular space on the floor that would be crowded if all players were inside it. Divide the group in half. One group stands just outside the boundary, facing into the circle. The other group stands just inside the circle facing out and directly opposite one player on the outside. They are now paired, so if there are ten players there will be five pairs. These pairs remain the same for the whole game. The object of the game is for one player to tag the other player with whom she is paired.

Count down from three, two, one, and the game begins.

The players on the outside of the circle (player #1) step into the circle and try to tag the player (player #2) with whom they are paired. Player #2 uses the crowd and tries to avoid getting tagged. NO RUNNING. Everyone must be careful to not bump into another person. Anytime anyone bumps into any other player they must stop, shake hands, and say, "I'm so, so sorry. It will never happen again."

If player #1 does manage to tag player #2, then player #2 must stop on that spot, twirl with their hand in the air (finger pointing upward), and say three times, "I've been tagged, I've been tagged, I've been tagged."

This action gives player #1 time to get away and "hide" in the crowd. At this point they switch, and player #2 is then the tagger and chases player #1. When tagged, player #1 says "I've been tagged, I've been tagged, I've been tagged" three times, and so the game continues.

Special Hints:
A rope makes an excellent boundary marker. The size of the boundary is critical and must ensure that players can move around one another safely but, at the same time, are very likely to bump into one another.

The facilitator or monitor is careful that no one runs or steps outside the circle. You can discover much about students by pairing them judiciously.

Group Weave

Activity Level: 2   **Age Level: 4+**
Location: Inside or outside   **Group Size: 4+**
Materials: An abundance of scarf lengths (or long strips) of fabrics of varying textures, sizes, and colors.

Game Description:
Players can do anything they want with the fabric as long as they are weaving with it. This includes running around one another or between one another and making a kinetic weave, placing the fabric on the ground in a stationary weave, or anything their imaginations allow.

Variations:
Endless, including adding (or limiting) different fabrics, colors, lengths. Play music during the weaving.

You can ask players to weave without using words (in silence).

Special Hints:
No right or wrong weaves. You may have to demonstrate weaving to the uninitiated.

Nature Designs

Activity Level: 2   **Age Level:** 6+
Location: Outside   **Group Size:** 2+
Materials: What nature provides

Game Description:
Objective: Each player creates a work of "art" out of natural objects.

Ask all players to walk around the area and observe colorful natural objects (such as branches, twigs, rocks). They can collect these natural objects to create their art piece. Each person then choses a locale (spot in nature), around which they create their work of art.

Give them a time limit and then invite the group to gather and walk around together to look at each creation.

Variations:
Name a theme, such as a geometric or circular design or animal habitats. Limit the kind or number of objects to be used (e.g., only rocks). Works of art can be limited to certain dimensions (e.g., has to be 2 feet high, or within a 3-foot square). Use groups of varying sizes for collaborative expression. Ask players to create a story to guide their work, or provide one for them.

Special Hints:
Demonstrate to stimulate those who have difficulty getting started. Visit each effort; ask questions, but do not offer advice unless asked to.

Come Together

Activity Level: 2   **Age Level: 5+**
Location: Inside or outside   **Group Size: 2**

Game Description:
Two players stand at opposite ends of a room, then run toward each other and leap. The object is to land as close as possible without touching one another.

Variations:
Land side by side. Shake hands while passing in the air. Turn around in the air and land close together.

Special Hints:
Needs several practice attempts before it becomes a game. Be careful.

Snowblind

Activity Level: 2   **Age Level: 5+**
Location: Inside or outside   **Group Size: 5**
Materials: A long foam sword or suitable padded substitute

Game Description:
It is blindfolded and has the sword, and chants for 10 seconds. The rest of the players run inside the boundaries and assume stationary crouch when the chanting stops. It moves around trying to tag players with the sword.

Variations:
Players stay still after chant stops. Anyone tagged joins It and next round begins with the Its chanting and players moving.

Special Hints:
Make sure sword is soft. Modify boundaries according to the abilities of the players.

Lemonade

Activity Level: 2   **Age Level: 4+**
Location: Inside or outside   **Group Size: 8**

Game Description:

Two teams, each with a safety area about 20 feet behind them, face off in the middle. One team has decided on the role (e.g., astronauts, clowns, scuba divers, etc.) they are going to pantomime. When someone guesses right, the pantomimists race for their safety area. The other team chases. Anyone tagged switches teams. No guesses for the first 30 seconds of the pantomime.

Variations:

Include scenes from nature, literature, or fantasy roles (e.g., clouds).

Special Hints:

Help the little ones. Everyone loves this game; it brings groups together.

Hawk and Mouse

Activity Level: 2   **Age Level: 6+**
Location: Inside or outside   **Group Size: 6**
Materials: Bell

Game Description:

Two blindfolded children are in the middle of the circle. One is a local predator, the other is its prey. The rest of the children keep them safely in the circle. The predator tries to find the prey who has a little bell around her neck. No talking.

Variations:

Anytime predator makes its sound, prey must answer.

Special Hints:

Make the circle smaller if the predator has trouble finding the prey. Remind the children not to let anyone fall.

Amigos All

Activity Level: 2   **Age Level: 5+**
Location: Inside or outside   **Group Size: 7**
Materials: Beanbags

Game Description:
Children walk at their own pace balancing a beanbag on their head. Leader controls the pace. If beanbag falls, the child is frozen. Another child must pick up the beanbag and place it on the frozen child's head, without losing her own.

Variations:
Many movements. Introduce obstacles. Cooperative relay race. Use music. Give children an opportunity to lead and come up with their own variations.

Special Hints:
If too difficult, let little ones use one hand.

Don't Use Your Teeth

Activity Level: 2   **Age Level: 6+**
Location: Outside   **Group Size: 3**
Materials: Tube sock or old towel

Game Description:
One player stands a short distance from the other two and throws a knotted sock or towel toward them. They have to catch it with their bodies, but without using their hands.

Variations:
Back to back. One of the two catchers closes her eyes.

Special Hints:
A good way to let active children who are having trouble being together work it out.

Up and Over

Activity Level: 2   **Age Level: 5+**
Location: Inside or outside   **Group Size: 10**

Game Description:

Divide the children into small groups of various sizes. Each group makes itself into a human obstacle. Players then have to run the course. When they get to an obstacle, the obstacle tells them how to get past it. As players pass an obstacle, they join the end of the line and traverse remaining obstacles. Each group finishes the course, it makes a new obstacle while all other players are still on previous obstacles. It can go on this way for hours.

Variations:

Add nonhuman obstacles. Allow no talking. Increase number of people comprising each obstacle. Add skills such as dribbling a ball while running the course.

Special Hints:

Watch carefully and learn about your players; much is revealed in this activity.

Standing Together

Activity Level: 2   **Age Level: 8+**
Location: Inside or outside   **Group Size: 4**

Game Description:

Seated in a circle, players grasp arms or hands and try to collectively stand up.

Variations:

Larger groups. Grabbing people not next to one another.

Special Hints:

Let the group experiment. Go slowly; the more people, the harder it is.

Octopus

Activity Level: 2   **Age Level: 4+**
Location: Inside or outside   **Group Size: 5**

Game Description:
In a defined area, one child is the Octopus. He attempts to tag another. When he does, that child is frozen but can wave her arms like the tentacles of an octopus, helping tag others until all are Octopi.

Variations:
All the tag variations. Vary play area size and location.

Special Hints:
Use big boundaries.

Beam Walk

Activity Level: 2   **Age Level: 5+**
Location: Inside or outside   **Group Size: 1**

Game Description:
Children practice on balance beams, such as on supported 4×4s. Many cooperative possibilities to try.

Variations:
Music, obstacles, pairs, etc.

Special Hints:
Be safe! Builds self-esteem if approached gently.

Walking Together

Activity Level: 2
Location: Outside
Materials: 2 ten-foot long
2×4" studs; 12 four-inch long leather straps or
nylon webbing; screws

Age Level: 8+
Group Size: 3–6 (depending on
size of the board with straps)

Game Description:

Six leather straps — for footholds — are screwed into each
stud. Six people slip their feet into the straps — left feet in
one "sandal," right feet in the other — and try to walk as a
unit.

Variations:

Move over or through obstacles. Dance. Move sideways. Try
indoors with pieces of carpet. Try various lengths of studs.

Special Hints:

Make sure they practice before trying difficult maneuvers.
Be safe.

Base Ball Pass

Activity Level: 2   **Age Level: 7+**
Location: Outside   **Group Size: 8**
Materials: Large balls

Game Description:
Four players and one large ball start at each of four bases.
Two players move their ball to the next base without using
hands and pass the ball to the waiting pair. They then await
the next pair coming behind them to pass them another
ball, which they move to the next base and pass on.

Variations:
Three on a team. Vary number of bases.

Special Hints:
Keep the game moving. Help the slower ones.

Moving Ladder

Activity Level: 2   **Age Level: 6+**
Location: Outside   **Group Size: 6**
Materials: Sturdy ladder

Game Description:
Players spread out along both sides of the ladder and lift
it so that it is held horizontally at their waists. One end is
lowered and the Traveler crawls on to it. The ladder is raised
and the Traveler crawls the length of the ladder.

Variations:
Use a plank. Change the angle of the ladder. Walk the ladder
around.

Special Hints:
Watch for tiring ladder holders and for show-offs.

Snake in the Grass

Activity Level: 2　　　　　　**Age Level: 5+**
Location: Inside or outside　　**Group Size: 5**

Game Description:
One player is the Snake in the grass, and lies and slithers around on her belly. All the other players touch one part of the Snake's body. When ready, trying to surprise the other players, the Snake says "Snake in the grass!" and tries to tag players. Anyone tagged becomes a Snake, until all are tagged.

Variations:
Change boundaries. Allow Snakes to be Alligators or Bears (move on hands and knees).

Special Hints:
Shoes off if possible. Keep the players challenging the Snake.

Log Pass

Activity Level: 2　　　　**Age Level: 7+**
Location: Outside　　　　**Group Size: 8**
Materials: Big log

Game Description:
Each player gets a number, starting with one. Players line up on a log in order. Now Player 1 must switch places with the last player (from the other end), without falling off the log. Then Player 2 switches places with the next-to-last player, and so on, until all have switched.

Variations:
Try with various conditions, for instance no talking, switchers blindfolded or one hand on top of head, etc.

Special Hints:
Make instructions clear at the beginning. Be safe!

Shape Tag

Activity Level: 2   **Age Level: 6+**
Location: Outside   **Group Size: 5**

Game Description:
Three players form a triangle. A fourth is It and a fifth tries to avoid being tagged. The triangle protects the fifth by changing shapes.

Variations:
Make play area boundaries with no tagging across the triangle. Players making triangle keep hands on each other's shoulders. Try multiple triangles with equal number of chasers and chased. Let any chaser catch anyone being chased.

Special Hints:
Change boundaries so no one is It for too long. Shape Tag can slip into competitiveness, so be careful.

Wheelbarrow

Activity Level: 2   **Age Level: 6+**
Location: Inside or outside   **Group Size: 2+**

Game Description:
In pairs, one child holds both legs of the other while that child moves on his hands.

Variations:
Choreograph movements of one or several pairs. Introduce obstacles, blindfolds, etc.

Special Hints:
Make sure each goes at their own speed. Switch partners.

Cooperative Juggle

Activity Level: 2   **Age Level: 8+**
Location: Inside or outside   **Group Size: 5**
Materials: Balls

Game Description:

Player 1 throws ball to any other player. The receiver says her name as she catches it. She then throws to another, who after saying his name, throws it to another, until all have had one chance. As the ball goes around a second time, the thrower says the name of the person to whom she is throwing. Players throw to same person each time. Keep adding balls to see how many can be juggled. Each time a ball is thrown, the thrower must call the name of the receiver. Player 1 initiates each ball.

Variations:

Large groups or small. Use yarn, socks, or anything soft. Cooperative Juggle is group juggling with many objects being thrown to everyone; all the thrower has to do is establish eye contact with the receiver.

Special Hints:

Good icebreaker; lots of fun. Let those having conflict play by themselves with many balls.

Garden

Activity Level: 2   **Age Level: 1+**
Location: Outside   **Group Size: 1**
Materials: Compost; fertilizers; shovels; seeds; soil;
water; fencing (if necessary)

Game Description:
Make an organic garden of whatever size is appropriate. Make it as a family, school, group, class, or community effort.

Variations:
Herb gardens. Seed gardens. Sprout gardens. Wildflower gardens.

Special Hints:
Grow something year round.

One Big Slug

Activity Level: 2   **Age Level: 4+**
Location: Inside or outside   **Group Size: 4**
Materials: Mats, things for an obstacle course

Game Description:
Children build an obstacle course. Then they connect into groups of four and, while holding the ankles of the one in front, go through the course on hands and knees.

Variations:
Cover all their bodies but heads with a blanket.

Cooperative Musical Chairs

Activity Level: 2 **Age Level: 3+**
Location: Inside or outside **Group Size: 5**
Materials: Music and floor pillows

Game Description:

Just like musical chairs, except that when the music stops and one pillow is removed, the remaining players all have to sit or touch the remaining pillows.

Variations:

Have all players sit on top of one another. Be careful that no one gets hurt.

Popcorn Balls

Activity Level: 2 **Age Level: 3+**
Location: Inside or outside **Group Size: 7**

Game Description:

Children crouch on the floor. Everyone chants: "Popcorn balls, popcorn balls, popcorn balls," sounding like a locomotive. Adult tells the children that as the pan (the floor) starts to heat up, the popcorn (the children) starts popping (children popping) all over the place. When two children bump each other while popping, they stick together. The game is over when all are one ball.

Special Hints:

Good for the little ones.

See Saw

Activity Level: 2   **Age Level: 8+**
Location: Inside or outside   **Group Size: 2**

Game Description:
Facing one another, partners sit with knees bent up and bottoms of their feet on the floor. They slip their feet just under the other's behind, join hands, and move by back and forward rocking motion.

Variations:
Reverse directions. Make it a co-op relay race. Use obstacles.

Special Hints:
End by coming to a standing position.

Rope Raising

Activity Level: 2   **Age Level: 8+**
Location: Inside or outside   **Group Size: 10**
Materials: Long rope tied at its ends to form a circle

Game Description:
Children sit in a circle, shoulder to shoulder. They can be on haunches if easier. Place the rope in a circle on the floor in front of them. Make the rope circle smaller than the children's circle so that there will be tension on it when they pull. Everyone pulls on the rope as they try to stand, all at the same time. Seated in a circle, group all pulls on the rope with their hands, so that they can all stand at once.

Variations:
Children try to stand in sequence rather than all at once.

Special Hints:
Coach the children to pull together. Watch out for the energetic children criticizing the less active ones.

Rolling Along

Activity Level: 2   **Age Level: 3+**
Location: Inside or outside   **Group Size: 2**

Game Description:

In pairs, partners lie stretched out on the floor, toe to toe, heads in opposite direction. They attempt to roll across the floor, keeping toes connected.

Variations:

Only toes of one foot connected. Try while sitting in an "L" position.

Special Hints:

Keep sending one pair down after the last. Use verbal encouragement. Select pairs carefully.

Dolphin and Fish

Activity Level: 2   **Age Level: 5+**
Location: Inside or outside   **Group Size: 8**

Game Description:

All but two players circle and hold hands. One free player is a Dolphin and the other is a Fish. Dolphin chases Fish. When Fish runs through the circle, children raise their arms; but when Dolphin tries to get through, they lower them.

Special Hints:

No favoritism among the children. Help the slow by altering the rules.

All of Us, All at Once

Activity Level: 2
Location: Inside or outside
Materials: Anything and everything

Age Level: 1+
Group Size: 2

Game Description:
Leader suggests a thing to be, and the group "is" that thing collectively.

Variations:
As varied as your imagination.

Special Hints:
Perfect for integrating new people and different ages.

Blind Trail

Activity Level: 2
Location: Outside
Materials: Rope and blindfolds

Age Level: 8+
Group Size: 6

Game Description:
Blindfolded players are guided through a part of the forest by feeling their way along a rope that has been placed there by the leader. The leader removes the rope when players get to the end. Players uncover their eyes and find their way back to the starting point.

Variations:
Across level areas, a stream, over logs. If players are old enough, use a very long rope.

Special Hints:
Emphasize calm awareness. Vary complexity.

Dances of the Mind

Activity Level: 2   **Age Level: 3+**
Location: Inside or outside   **Group Size: 3+**

Game Description:

Have the children form a dance as an expression of a chosen concept, for instance high-low and medium.

Variations:

Colors. Time. Relatives, aggressions, etc. Use music as appropriate. Let the older ones pick their own.

Special Hints:

Help them along. Filter sarcasm. Once in progress, a great builder of self-esteem and nonverbal communication skills.

Activity Level 3

Group Poem

Activity Level: 3   **Age Level: 8+**
Location: Outside   **Group Size: 6+**
Materials: Paper, pencils or pens

Game Description:

Go to a place in nature, preferably after a hike. Gather the group. Ask them to sit quietly and observe everything around them. Remind them to listen to all the sounds. If appropriate, ask them to close their eyes for a while. Then, giving them only one minute, ask them to write three or four words describing their setting. Gather the pieces of paper.

After gathering all papers, read the words aloud. Be sure to say each word clearly, with inflection, so that they become a poem when strung together.

Variations:

Have one of the players do the reading.

You can limit the descriptors to colors or to sounds. Prior to this activity, you can do the hike in silence. Ask them to make the reading into a melody after words are spoken.

Special Hints:

Read in a considered manner, and treat your reading seriously. Pause slightly when it feels appropriate, but keep a cadence.

The Signs Are Everywhere

Activity Level: 3   **Age Level: 8+**
Location: Inside   **Group Size: 15+**
Materials: To be determined by the players

Game Description:

Divide players into groups of approximately five players. Each group devises its own nonverbal messaging system. In preparation, the facilitator can refer to the Navy semaphores as an example. No drawings of anything specific. No charades-type gestures. Players can ask for materials to help create their own visual alphabet. Their created message should be at least two sentences. When everyone is ready, usually about 30–45 minutes, each group takes a turn communicating their message — using their symbols, signs, flags, etc. After it has been demonstrated twice, the players watching can try to guess the message.

Special Hints:

If there is difficulty getting this activity started, remind the players that they can use their bodies to form letters. Offer suggestions when necessary. This can be a challenging activity for those who have difficulty conveying information using written words. At the same time, others may find it easier to communicate without written words or the alphabet.

Add a dimension by including gibberish sounds. However, the sounds can refer to letters or syllables, not whole words.

What Does This Mean?

Activity Level: 3   **Age Level: 5+**
Location: Inside or outside   **Group Size: 4**
Materials: Anything and everything

Game Description:
Each player is told to find an object that has a special value for her. Discussion follows during which each child tells how the object exemplifies her value. For example, a rock represents friendship because of its solidity, or the moon is caring due to lighting the earth at night.

Variations:
Restrict objects to nature. Agree on one value for the entire class and have everyone find different representations of it.

Special Hints:
Give examples.
Encourage free expression.
Participate yourself.

Where Were You?

Activity Level: 3   **Age Level: 5+**
Location: Inside or outside   **Group Size: 12**

Game Description:
Leader stands in the middle. Children are in four teams on her left, right, in front, and behind. Children are still while leader turns in a circle and stops. Then teams reposition themselves as they were before — on the left, right, front, and back.

Variations:
Collectively time them.

Special Hints:
Best to have 16 or 20 children.

Rhythm Sticks

Activity Level: 3   **Age Level: 6+**
Location: Inside or outside   **Group Size: 2**
Materials: Cut one-inch dowels about 18" long

Game Description:
Children sit cross-legged facing one another. They establish a rhythm with their sticks by hitting their own sticks together, hitting the floor, hitting each other's sticks. Then, do it to music.

Variations:
Vary group size. Use one hand only. Let the children sing their own music. Try it blindfolded.

Special Hints:
Play along and have fun. Vary the ages playing together. Let some children make music with other instruments. Enhances musical and nonverbal communication skills.

Still Photograph

Activity Level: 3   **Age Level: 8+**
Location: Inside or outside   **Group Size: 4**

Game Description:
One player takes a few members of the group and tells them of an experience when she was happy. She then places them in a frozen picture recalling that time. The rest of the group has to guess the situation.

Variations:
Other emotions. Vary group size. Share tableaux with the larger group.

Special Hints:
Encourage detail. Stimulates compassion. Group children having difficulty together. Cannot use Christmas or birthday for the photo.

Wheel

Activity Level: 3
Location: Inside or outside

Age Level: 4+
Group Size: 5

Game Description:

All players stand sideways in a circle and put hands toward the middle. They are now spokes of a wheel. Turn and move around the room.

Variations:

Hopping and/or skipping. Over obstacles. Eyes closed.

Special Hints:

Increase complexity to keep interest high. Best for the very young.

Stiff As a Board

Activity Level: 3
Location: Inside or outside

Age Level: 5+
Group Size: 5

Game Description:

One player lies on the ground as stiffly as possible. The others pick her up and carry her as far as they can.

Variations:

Make it a relay race. Introduce obstacles. Balance a glass of water on the back of the one being carried.

Special Hints:

Make sure no one is straining. No jokes or put-downs about another child's body shape.

Down the Tube

Activity Level: 3   **Age Level: 5+**
Location: Inside or outside   **Group Size: 2**
Materials: Ping pong ball, cardboard tube such as from toilet tissue roll

Game Description:
Toss the ball back and forth, trying to catch it in the tube.

Variations:
Use a ring instead of ping pong ball and try to catch it on a stick. Vary distance between players or hand used in game.

Down the Hole

Activity Level: 3   **Age Level: 5+**
Location: Inside or outside   **Group Size: 6**
Materials: Old sheet or bedspread and a ball

Game Description:
Cut a small hole, just big enough for the ball, in the center of the sheet. Children hold the edges of the sheet and try to get the ball to go through the hole.

Variations:
Use several balls, try a parachute instead of a sheet.

Special Hints:
Great fun; brings the group to a "center."

Hello, But I'm Gone

Activity Level: 3

Age Level: 4+

Location: Inside or outside

Group Size: 7

Game Description:

Children sit in a circle with one standing on the outside. She pats someone on the head and each runs in opposite directions around the circle. When they meet they must stop, shake hands and say "Hello, but I'm gone." The first player runs and sits down and the second proceeds around the circle and repeats the game.

Special Hints:

Great fun for the little ones.

Use That Rope

Activity Level: 3

Age Level: 3+

Location: Inside or outside

Group Size: 4

Materials: Rope

Game Description:

Using jump ropes, children make letters, numbers, geometric shapes, flowers, etc.

Variations:

Change size of rope. Vary number of children and ways in which rope shapes interrelate.

Special Hints:

Fade into background, but stay close to help maintain flow.

Alternate Leaning

Activity Level: 3   **Age Level: 6+**
Location: Inside or outside   **Group Size: 20**

Game Description:
Stand in a circle with arms linked. Alternate people are "ins" and "outs." At the signal, players lean either in or out. By supporting one another, a steep lean can be achieved.

Variations:
Hold hands. Do it in rhythm.

Special Hints:
Keep feet stationary. The more people the better.

Hold Me Up

Activity Level: 3   **Age Level: 7+**
Location: Inside or outside   **Group Size: 2**

Game Description:
Partners face off and then slowly fall away and catch one another by the arm — pull up close and then fall away again and catch by another part of the arm.

Variations:
One arm or two arms. Try groups of three or four.

Special Hints:
Go slow and make sure all are comfortable.

How Many Are Standing?

Activity Level: 3
Location: Inside or outside

Age Level: 4+
Group Size: 8

Game Description:
Sit in a circle. Anyone stands up whenever they want to, but cannot remain standing longer than five seconds. Aim of the game is to have exactly four standing at one time.

Variations:
Vary group size and amount standing, or time standing up.

Special Hints:
Great for an icebreaker and for the little ones.

Feeling Sculpture

Activity Level: 3
Location: Inside or outside

Age Level: 8+
Group Size: 4

Game Description:
Partner A whispers a feeling word into partner B's ear. B sculpts A into a representation of that feeling. After one minute they find another pair. Each pair tries to guess the other's feeling. Add charades if necessary.

Variations:
Do it in groups.

Special Hints:
Don't forget to shape the face.

Strike the Pose

Activity Level: 3
Location: Inside or outside

Age Level: 6+
Group Size: 8

Game Description:
Two leave the room. The rest of the group decides on a pose that is specific but not too detailed. The two come back in and begin striking poses. The group signals hot or cold until the two strike the group pose.

Variations:
Only one leaves the room.

Special Hints:
Vary pose complexity according to age level. Many moves should be tried at first until the group reacts.

Spaghetti

Activity Level: 3
Location: Inside or outside

Age Level: 6+
Group Size: 6

Game Description:
All stand in a circle. Join hands, but not with the person on either side. Now untangle without letting go of hands.

Special Hints:
Sometimes it cannot be done. Give all a chance to move people around. See introduction.

Find Your Animal Mate

Activity Level: 3   **Age Level: 3+**
Location: Inside or outside   **Group Size: 8**

Game Description:

Animal names are written on a piece of paper. Each animal is named twice. The children are each given a slip so they know only their animal. They then act out the animal, while trying to find their partner. When two find each other, they ask the leader if they are right.

Variations:

Without sounds.

Gyrating Reptile

Activity Level: 3   **Age Level: 4+**
Location: Inside or outside   **Group Size: 5**

Game Description:

Children lie on the floor and grab the ankles of the child in front of them, making one big snake. Then, gyrating energetically, they try to move across the floor.

Variations:

Over obstacles. Against time.

Special Hints:

Ask the children for ideas.

Nature Acting

Activity Level: 3   **Age Level: 3+**
Location: Inside or outside   **Group Size: 4**

Game Description:
A child acts out a real life situation, e.g., a butterfly drinking from a flower; or a teacher reprimanding a student. The others try to guess what it is.

Variations:
Use props. Let children act in groups.

Special Hints:
Encourage children to come up with their own ideas, but be there to help. Don't let anyone make fun by putting down another.

Animal Acting

Activity Level: 3   **Age Level: 3+**
Location: Inside or outside   **Group Size: 5**

Game Description:
Children choose an animal and act it out. Others try to guess what it is.

Variations:
Have the animal doing something. Use sounds.

Special Hints:
Let the children choose their own animals, if possible.

Tied Together

Activity Level: 3   **Age Level:** 5+
Location: Inside or outside   **Group Size:** 6

Game Description:
Two children hide their eyes. The others join hands and make themselves into the craziest knot they can. The two open their eyes and try to undo the knot without breaking handholds.

Variations:
Eyes closed.

Special Hints:
Make sure all get a chance to be the undoers.

Blind Walks

Activity Level: 3   **Age Level:** 6+
Location: Inside or outside   **Group Size:** 2
Materials: Blindfolds

Game Description:
In pairs, with one blindfolded, the children lead one another.

Variations:
Obstacles. Do it in nature.

Special Hints:
Builds self-esteem to trust and be trusted. Instruct to be careful.

Face to Face

Activity Level: 3   **Age Level: 3+**
Location: Inside or outside   **Group Size: 2**

Game Description:
Partners stand a couple of feet apart. One closes her eyes and gently moves forward, trying to connect noses. The other stands still.

Variations:
Both have eyes closed.

Special Hints:
Good for special relationships. Introduce breathing as a clue.

In and Out

Activity Level: 3   **Age Level: 5+**
Location: Inside or outside   **Group Size: 2**

Game Description:
Partners face one another with feet spread to shoulder width. With hands up, palms open, bodies rigid, the partners lean forward and catch one another. Then push off and spring back up.

Variations:
Vary distance to limit of capabilities.

Special Hints:
Play on soft surface. Match players consciously.

Rhythm Learning

Activity Level: 3 **Age Level: 6+**
Location: Inside or outside **Group Size: 2**
Materials: Large ball

Game Description:
In pairs, children pass a ball back and forth while calling out letters of the alphabet.

Variations:
Spell words. Names of animals or familiar people. Do simple mathematics.

Special Hints:
Keep a rhythm going, perhaps by handclapping, but do not make it too fast or exclude anyone.

Use That Body

Activity Level: 3 **Age Level: 4+**
Location: Inside or outside **Group Size: 4**

Game Description:
Together, the children make numbers, shapes, letters with their bodies. Everyone in the group must be included.

Special Hints:
Use small groups.

Move Softly

Activity Level: 3   **Age Level: 8+**
Location: Inside or outside   **Group Size: 6**
Materials: Blindfold and a rag for treasure

Game Description:
One child sits on the ground, blindfolded, guarding a treasure with the referee standing behind her. She "falls asleep" — wearing a blindfold — and the others try to creep up as quietly as possible to steal the treasure. If the child hears someone, she points in that direction and everyone freezes. If the referee agrees that the child guarding the treasure pointed directly at the person, that person must take three steps backward.

Special Hints:
Be the referee, or allow a child to be the referee.

No-Hands Ball Pass

Activity Level: 3   **Age Level: 5+**
Location: Inside or outside   **Group Size: 5**
Materials: Ball

Game Description:
Players sit on floor in tight circle and extend feet towards the center. A ball is placed on one player's lap. The idea is to move the ball around the circle as fast as possible without using hands.

Variations:
Vary the size and number of balls. Reverse the direction of the ball.

Special Hints:
Lots of fun. If it doesn't work the first time, try again.

Pasta

Activity Level: 3   **Age Level: 3+**
Location: Inside   **Group Size: 6**

Game Description:

Players are a package of pasta, bundled close together. As pot boils, players begin to relax and eventually end up in a limp pile on the floor.

Blanket Toss

Activity Level: 3   **Age Level: 6+**
Location: Inside or outside   **Group Size: 6**
Materials: Balloons and a blanket

Game Description:

Cut a hole that is the size of a balloon in the middle of the blanket. Place balloons on it. Players grab edges of the blanket and try to maneuver the balloon through the hole.

Variations:

Can keep score, with smaller values given to smaller balloons and larger values given to larger balloons.

Special Hints:

Join the fun!

Strange Positions

Activity Level: 3   **Age Level: 4+**
Location: Inside   **Group Size: 5**

Game Description:
The leader tells players to get into a strange position and hold
it. The leader then tells them to get into a second strange
position, and so on. Positions should involve more than one
player.

Special Hints:
For the very young.

Wooden Children

Activity Level: 3   **Age Level: 4+**
Location: Outside   **Group Size: 8**

Game Description:
Several players lie on their backs, totally stiff, being logs.
Others cooperate to lift these logs and place them as corner
poles for a house, or put them in a stove. Players huddle in
house or warm themselves around stove.

Variations:
Other pole applications. Other players dig imaginary holes
for posts. Talk about the many gifts trees give us.

Shoe Mates

Activity Level: 3
Location: Inside
Materials: Shoes

Age Level: 6+
Group Size: 12

Game Description:
Players take off shoes and pile them in the middle. Each player selects an unmatched pair of shoes, neither of which are her own. All walk around trying to find shoe mates and stand next to people so that shoes are matched in pairs.

Special Hints:
Remind big people to be careful to not crush little toes.

Rocks in a Creek

Activity Level: 3
Location: Inside or outside

Age Level: 4+
Group Size: 8

Game Description:
Players put hands on hips and slowly spin "downstream" together. As elbows touch, arms go down, simulating wearing down of sharp edges. Dizzy players crouch at bottom of creek, face upstream, extend arms back and wiggle open hands like rippling water.

Special Hints:
Talk about water as energy, transporting and rounding rocks.

Ocean Friends

Activity Level: 3   **Age Level: 3+**
Location: Inside or outside   **Group Size: 8**
Materials: Beanbags

Game Description:
Fill rooms with (imaginary) water. Players swim around with beanbags on heads. Dropped bag means player freezes. Friend must take deep breath, hold nose, dive down and replace bag. End by pulling plug and all whirlpool closer and closer to center.

Variations:
Practice deep breaths before starting. Children may use one finger to hold beanbag on.

Hold That Floor

Activity Level: 3   **Age Level: 4+**
Location: Inside   **Group Size: 5**

Game Description:
Players run around until leader calls "freeze," and a number. Players must stop and touch the number of body parts to the floor that the leader called.

Variations:
When "freeze" is called, players have to find a partner and get the body parts down together.

Slow Motion Tag

Activity Level: 3   **Age Level: 5+**
Location: Inside or outside   **Group Size: 12**

Game Description:
Slow motion tag. When tagged, a person joins It. When
4 players are joined as It, they split into pairs and tag others.
When everyone is tagged, all chant "A-moe-ba,"
so all will know that the game is over.

Variations:
Vary the split size of the It group, with overall number of
players.

Special Hints:
Remember — move in slow motion.

A Chance to Be Nice

Activity Level: 3   **Age Level: 3+**
Location: Inside or outside   **Group Size: 8+**

Game Description:
Players line up facing one another. Taking turns each player skips down the line while the others say something nice
about that person.

Special Hints:
Make sure no sarcasm surfaces. Wait until your group begins to feel good about one another. Come back to it later
if it fails the first time. An easy way to say something nice
about someone else.

Whose Shoe?

Activity Level: 3   **Age Level: 6+**
Location: Inside   **Group Size: 5**
Materials: Shoes

Game Description:
Each child takes off one shoe and puts it in a pile. Everyone picks up someone else's shoe and, while somehow holding it, joins hands and forms a circle. Shoe owners are identified and shoes must be returned while holding hands.

Inuit Ball Pass

Activity Level: 3   **Age Level: 8+**
Location: Inside or outside   **Group Size: 8**
Materials: Ball

Game Description:
Players kneel in a circle and pass the ball from person to person with a flat, open hand (palm up). The aim is to move the ball as rapidly as possible around the circle without actually grasping it.

Variations:
Use more than one ball at a time.

Special Hints:
Learn to play with two hands first.

Don't Let Go

Activity Level: 3 **Age Level: 5+**
Location: Inside or outside **Group Size: 2**

Game Description:
Partners face off, extend arms, and hold hands. Now move into positions that would leave each partner totally off-balance were it not for the support of the other.

Variations:
Support with different parts than hands. Try with more than two people.

Special Hints:
Tell each player to explore all kinds of new positions. Quiet music is nice. Builds trust.

Children's Carapace

Activity Level: 3 **Age Level: 3+**
Location: Inside **Group Size: 5**
Materials: Blanket and tarp or gym mat

Game Description:
Each member of the group gets on its hands and knees. Place the blanket or tarp over the whole group (to simulate a turtle shell). Working together they try to move a large shell (blanket) in one direction.

Variations:
Over an obstacle. Play out turtle stories.

Special Hints:
Give them time to realize they all need to move in the same direction.

Jump Jump Jump

Activity Level: 3 **Age Level: 3+**
Location: Outside **Group Size: 5**

Game Description:
Each child jumps in succession, taking off from where the last person in their group landed. The aim is to see how far the group can collectively jump.

Variations:
Over obstacles. Estimate the jumps to a certain spot.

Special Hints:
Vary the order in which children jump. Encourage them to beat their old mark.

All Paint

Activity Level: 3 **Age Level: 4+**
Location: Inside **Group Size: 6**
Materials: Large paper and paint

Game Description:
A shape is drawn on a large piece of paper. The paper is hung at a height such that the tallest in the group must jump her highest to reach the top of the shape. Children dip their fingers in paint and, jumping up, try to fill the shape in with colour.

Variations:
Use letters or numbers as shapes.

Special Hints:
Vary heights in each group, making sure the shortest gets the bottom to fill. Teaches nonverbal sharing.

Probably Wet

Activity Level: 3   **Age Level: 6+**
Location: Outside   **Group Size: 6**
Materials: Cups and water

Game Description:
Players stand in a circle with an empty paper cup in their teeth. One cup is filled with water, and players attempt to pass the water from cup to cup without spilling it. No hands.

Variations:
Fill more cups. Widen the circle.

Special Hints:
Make sure it is OK with each child to get wet.

Handle With Care

Activity Level: 3   **Age Level: 4+**
Location: Outside   **Group Size: 5**
Materials: Big leaves

Game Description:
Players stand in line. A broad leaf is passed overhead until it reaches the back of the line. Then, that person brings it to the front and starts again. The aim is for everyone to be first, and not to damage the leaf.

Variations:
Play it with any natural object.

Special Hints:
Talk about leaves. Discuss ecology, and/or the damage humans do to nature.

Marble Tracking

Activity Level: 3   **Age Level: 7+**
Location: Outside   **Group Size: 3**
Materials: PVC pipe and marbles

Game Description:
Cut 1" PVC pipe in half lengthwise to make a track. Use these tracks on a slope to make a downhill run for the marbles.

Variations:
Steep downhill. Slow switchbacks. Introduce obstacles.

Special Hints:
Help set it up. Participate yourself. Let the children make their own courses.

Path Finder

Activity Level: 3   **Age Level: 5+**
Location: Outside   **Group Size: 6**

Game Description:
Divide players into two groups. Each group marks their own nature trail using only natural objects. Dots of flour are OK, but do not deface anything. Meet back at starting place and then each group follows the other's trail.

Variations:
Vary the terrain, including through water.

Special Hints:
Don't let one group make it too hard for the other until the game has been played a few times. Builds children's confidence in natural settings.

Sounds and Colors

Activity Level: 3 **Age Level: 6+**
Location: Outside **Group Size: 4**

Game Description:
In a natural setting, children lie on their backs with eyes closed. Every time one hears a new bird call, they raise a finger. Then, looking around with eyes open, do the same for new colors.

Variations:
Use any sounds. See if they can count to ten without hearing a new call or seeing a new color.

Special Hints:
Emphasize quietness.

Tree Silhouettes

Activity Level: 3 **Age Level: 6+**
Location: Outside **Group Size: 5**

Game Description:
In a place where several different tree types grow, have a child shape herself like a tree. The others try to guess which tree she is imitating.

Variations:
Use groups. Do any natural formation.

Special Hints:
Can be worked in with real life drama.

Hug a Tree

Activity Level: 3   **Age Level: 5+**
Location: Outside   **Group Size: 2**
Materials: Blindfold

Game Description:

In pairs, one child leads another, who is blindfolded, to a tree by a circuitous route. The blindfolded one explores the tree with all other senses, and then is led back to the starting point. Blindfold removed, she sets out to find her tree.

Variations:

Hug anything.

Special Hints:

Try to find a heavily wooded area. Talk about trees.

Unnature Trail

Activity Level: 3   **Age Level: 6+**
Location: Outside   **Group Size: 6**
**Materials: Various unnatural objects, such as paper clips
or bobby pins**

Game Description:
Along a trail, hide a dozen human-made objects. Some should
be easy to find, others well hidden. The children try to find
them, but do not touch them. They report their findings to
the teacher, who sends them back to look for any they missed.

Special Hints:
Hide a paper bag well. It is unlikely it will be found, and will
facilitate a discussion about camouflage, which is one of the
aims of this activity.

Duplicate

Activity Level: 3   **Age Level: 8+**
Location: Outside   **Group Size: 4**
Materials: Naturally occurring objects and a cloth

Game Description:
Collect several naturally occurring objects from the game
area. Place them on the ground, covered by the cloth. Lifting
the cloth for 30 seconds, let the children study the objects,
then cover them again. Then, tell them to go find objects like
them in the area.

Variations:
Vary time to study. Vary number of objects.

Special Hints:
Pull objects out one at a time to see who has the match.
Careful not to let this game get competitive.

Prooie

Activity Level: 3   **Age Level: 7+**
Location: Inside or outside   **Group Size: 10**

Game Description:
Players scatter around a defined area. All close their eyes. Leader moves through the group and silently chooses one player to be "Prooie." Prooie opens her eyes. Leader gives a signal to begin. All except Prooie start wandering around, keeping their eyes closed. As they bump into each other, they say "Prooie?" If the person answers "Prooie," they separate and continue to wander. The object is to find the Prooie, who never answers back. When they bump into Prooie, ask their question, and receive no reply, they open their eyes and join hands with Prooie. Game continues until all are joined as Prooie.

Special Hints:
Make sure all keep their eyes closed. If game ends too quickly, expand boundaries.

Activity Level 4

Social Justice Ideals

Activity Level: 4   **Age Level: 9 to 16**
Location: Inside or outside   **Group Size: 6**

Game Description:

One player choses a few others and describes a scenario she feels is socially unjust. Together they choreograph the scenario according to the description. Then, she directs them to act it out in silence, with each team player contributing to the choreography.

There must be movement and feeling.

The other students just watch as the audience. Each small group presents their scenario two times.

Then, the facilitator gives the signal that the audience can try to guess what is happening.

Variations:

Give the player creating the scenario the choice of which partner to choose. Ask them to reflect on their experiences while observing. Include their reflections in post-presentation dialog.

Special Hints:

The facilitator cannot judge any offering, no matter what their personal persuasion might be. Using inquiry, allow each group to make their own values clarification.

Plant a Pet Pickle

Activity Level: 4   **Age Level: 4+**
Location: Inside or outside   **Group Size: 5**

Game Description:

Players come together into a circle. Each player takes a turn leading.

Leader calls out either "Plant," "Pet," or "Pickle" and adds a feeling or a sensation that comes to mind in the moment.

For example, the leader may call out "Dog, sad." He then acts out his version of a sad dog. At the same time, the others in the circle do their expression of a sad dog. If they don't have a pet, they imagine what it would be like to be sad dog.

It's a bit trickier with Plant, but prickly cacti and sweet smelling rose or soft grass are easy examples. Pickle, however, is a bit harder. Use your imagination.

I am sure the children will.

Variations:

Switch out pickle (if you must — some may find a pickle difficult to relate to).

Special Hints:

Give suggestions as often as needed. Facilitators must participate in the activity. Be prepared for much laughter.

Are We Near You?

Activity Level: 4
Location: Outside
Materials: Blindfold

Age Level: 7+
Group Size: 6

Game Description:

Best played on a narrow hiking trail. One child sent ahead on the trail until she is out of sight. She steps off the trail and sits, blindfolded. After she is settled, the leader starts the group walking. They walk slowly, carefully, and as silently as possible. *No talking.* The object of the game is for the group to secretly file past the blindfolded player. When the blindfolded player thinks she hears them she points and says aloud, "I hear you." Upon hearing the words, everyone freezes. The blindfolded child points to where she heard the sound. If she is close to someone, then the game ends and someone takes her place. If she misses, the group keeps moving. The blindfolded player can point three times in a turn.

Variations:

Have the blindfolded child cup her hands behind her ears to amplify sound. Group can file past one by one, or as a unit.

Special Hints:

The blindfolded child can be the prey; a deer, mouse, etc. The group are predators; coyote, hawk, humans, etc. Discuss both roles afterward. Often, the prey has feelings of being hunted. Group frustrations may surface if one or two make a noise which reveals the whole group.

What Animal Am I?

Activity Level: 4   **Age Level: 6+**
Location: Inside or outside   **Group Size: 5**
Materials: Pictures of animals and safety pins

Game Description:
A picture of a different animal is pinned to each player's back. The player asks yes or no questions of the other players and tries to guess the animal.

Variations:
Substitute environments, buildings, or people for animals.

Special Hints:
Start easy and make sure players circulate while asking questions.

Pinocchio

Activity Level: 4   **Age Level: 4+**
Location: Inside or outside   **Group Size: 2**

Game Description:
One partner is a puppet on the ground, unable to move. The other child is puppeteer and moves the child by pulling imaginary strings.

Special Hints:
Do a few practice turns so children get the feel. Vary partners. Subtle nonverbal communication skills enhanced.

Talking Without Words

Activity Level: 4   Age Level: 4+
Location: Inside or outside   Group Size: 2

Game Description:
One player makes nonsense sounds and the partner responds with a movement showing how the sound made her feel. A conversation develops.

Variations:
Do it in larger groups. Bring in props.

Special Hints:
Start with short interactions and let "vocabularies" build in time. Creates a new dimension in communication.

Rhythm Pulse

Activity Level: 4   Age Level: 6+
Location: Inside or outside   Group Size: 4

Game Description:
Group sits in a circle with hands joined. One person starts a pattern of squeezes in one direction. This pattern is a pulse. For example: 3 quick squeezes, followed by 2 long squeezes. The pulse is passed around the circle until it is back with the person who started it. Object is to keep the pulse from altering.

Special Hints:
No more than 8 people, so everyone has a chance to start a pulse before tiring of the game. Excellent for quieting and focusing energy. Good at the end of the day. If played with less than 5, use complicated pulses. Short discussion of each pulse can be interesting.

Hit the Nail

Activity Level: 4   **Age Level: 4+**
Location: Inside or outside   **Group Size: 4**
Materials: Board; hammer; nails

Game Description:
Start a nail in the board. Now each player takes one turn hitting the nail. See how few strokes the class can use to get the nail all the way in.

Variations:
Use the weaker arm. Try blindfolded. Vary nail size or hammer size. Apply the same principle to sawing through wood.

Special Hints:
Watch out for "machos." Make sure no one gets hurt.

Sleeper

Activity Level: 4   **Age Level: 7+**
Location: Inside or outside   **Group Size: 10**

Game Description:
Players cover eyes. Leader silently chooses Sleeper. Players open eyes and start to mingle. Sleeper puts a player to sleep by surreptitiously winking once at her. Player who was winked at counts silently to 3 and falls asleep on the floor. Play continues until someone guesses who the Sleeper is.

Variations:
Can be played sitting in a circle.

Special Hints:
Encourage players to look into each other's eyes. No guessing who Sleeper is until at least one person is asleep. Encourage players to be discreet with their winks. One guess per player as to who the Sleeper is.

Two Way Copy

Activity Level: 4   **Age Level: 4+**
Location: Inside or outside **Group Size: 2**

Game Description:

First, two children face one another. One moves and the other mirrors her movements. Next, one child stands behind the other. As the first one moves, the following child shadows the movements.

Variations:

Limit to facial movements. Allow movement in mirrors.

Special Hints:

Good for mixed ages. Older children will enjoy doing this with little ones. Do not let it become competitive. Vary partners.

In Between

Activity Level: 4   **Age Level: 3+**
Location: Inside or outside **Group Size: 2**
Materials: Large rubber ball or other objects, depending on variations

Game Description:

Two children face each other and balance a ball between their bodies without using their hands.

Variations:

Increase amount of players. Substitute other objects for the ball. Have players hold a board and balance objects on it. Let them walk around.

Special Hints:

Increase complexity to keep it interesting. Help the little ones. Do it yourself.

Find Your Rock

Activity Level: 4   **Age Level: 4+**
Location: Outside   **Group Size: 6**
Materials: A cloth to lay rocks on

Game Description:
Each player finds a special rock. Give them 4 minutes to get to know it using all senses. Place rocks on cloth or cleared surface. Group sits around rock pile. With their eyes closed, they try to find their rock by touch. When they believe they have theirs, they open their eyes to see if they are right.

Variations:
Place large cloth over rocks so they can search with eyes open. Add rocks that belong to nobody. Use other natural objects.

Special Hints:
At first, make suggestions as they feel their rocks: Warm? Smooth? Establish size limits so they are encouraged to notice characteristics other than size.

Clothes Switch

Activity Level: 4   **Age Level: 5+**
Location: Inside or outside   **Group Size: 2**
Materials: Large old shirt

Game Description:
One player wears a vary large old shirt. Partners hold hands. The aim is to get the shirt onto the second partner without letting go of the hands.

Special Hints:
Help the little ones. Let older ones having conflict try this one together.

I Am

Activity Level: 4   **Age Level: 5+**
Location: Inside or outside   **Group Size: 7**

Game Description:

All stand in a circle. Taking turns, each player goes to the middle and calls her name and makes a sound and movement. Then everyone imitates the person in the middle while she watches. Then the next person goes.

Variations:

If the group is close, have one child do the name of another person in the group.

Be an animal instead of yourself.

Special Hints:

Good for warm-up or introductions. Good for group re-centering.

Psychic Nonsense

Activity Level: 4   **Age Level: 5+**
Location: Inside or outside   **Group Size: 2**

Game Description:

Players decide on three sound and motion movements. One example of a sound and motion movement is flapping the arms and cawing like a crow. They then turn their backs to one another. On the count of three, they turn around and do one of the three movements. The aim is for everyone to do the same one.

Special Hints:

Join the fun!

Canyon Echo

Activity Level: 4   **Age Level: 5+**
Location: Outside   **Group Size: 4**

Game Description:

Group is on a trail, single file. First and last in line are the canyon walls. All the players in between are the canyon air that the echo travels through. The head of the line starts the echo. Echo can be any sound or noise pattern. The echo is passed from person to person down the canyon air until it hits the canyon wall, which is the last person in the line. The wall then starts a new and different echo which travels through the air to the head of the line again. After voicing the echo, person 1 steps off the trail and rejoins the line after it files past, becoming the end of the line, or the opposite canyon wall. The new lead person starts a new echo.

Variations:

Introduce a movement to go with the sound.

Special Hints:

Encourage many different sounds. Start game with story about canyons and echoes. Great for children who are getting tired or bored while hiking, for they begin to focus on one another rather than the discomfort. Keeps children from getting separated from the group.

Back to Back

Activity Level: 4   **Age Level: 4+**
Location: Inside or outside   **Group Size: 2**

Game Description:

Two children sit back to back and attempt to get up without using their hands.

Variations:

Vary group size.

Special Hints:

If difficult, suggest they link elbows. Let children in conflict try this together.

Chief

Activity Level: 4   **Age Level: 4+**
Location: Inside or outside   **Group Size: 8**

Game Description:

One player goes where she cannot see the others. A leader is chosen. She does a movement which the others follow. The leader changes the movement regularly. The others follow the leader's movement. The hidden one returns and by watching everyone tries to guess who the leader is.

Variations:

Send more than one away and have them confer. Limit the guesses. Have two leaders and switch off movements. Use movements that make no sound.

Special Hints:

Join the fun!

Catch Me

Activity Level: 4   **Age Level: 7+**
Location: Inside or outside   **Group Size: 7**

Game Description:
About seven children form a tight circle. One child in the middle stiffens her body and falls in any direction. The others catch her and gently push her around.

Variations:
Vary the rhythm of the passing.

Special Hints:
Make sure the children are attentive. Nice way to start the day.

Make Me Into You

Activity Level: 4   **Age Level: 6+**
Location: Inside or outside   **Group Size: 3**

Game Description:
One player closes their eyes. Another forms a sculptured pose. The one with their eyes closed sculpts the third player into the pose chosen by player two, based on sense of touch.

Special Hints:
No one has ever abused this game. Brings out the gentleness in people.

A What?

Activity Level: 4 **Age Level: 7+**
Location: Inside or outside **Group Size: 8**
Materials: Two balls

Game Description:

Players are in a circle. Player 1 hands a ball to Player 2 and says, "this is a banana." Player 2 asks, "a what?" "A banana," says Player 1. "Oh, a banana," says Player 2, who then hands the ball to Player 3 and says "This is a banana." Player 3 asks player 2, who asks player 1, "a what?" Player 1 answers player 2, who then turns to answer player 3, "a banana." Then player 3 passes the ball to player 4 and says "this is a banana." Player 4 asks player 3, who asks play 2, who asks player 1, "a what?" Player 1 answers player 2, who answers player 3, who answers player 4, "a banana." And so on around the circle one way.

While the "banana" goes around the circle clockwise, the other ball, a "pineapple," goes around the circle counter-clockwise, with the same verbal procedures.

Special Hints:

Practice a few times before judging this one. It always turns out to be great fun and a tension breaker. People will play it often to get it right, for it is hard to make both balls go all the way around. Make up silly names for the objects.

Cast Your Vote

Activity Level: 4   **Age Level: 5+**
Location: Inside or outside **Group Size: 6**

Game Description:
Draw a line on the ground that represents a continuum from "strongly agree" to "strongly disagree." Introduce topics and let children vote by where they stand. No talking.

Variations:
Use raising of hands or voice vote.

Special Hints:
Do not vote yourself. Make jokes. Include issues from classroom and family. Great for values clarification as it allows older children to express opinions on sensitive issues.

Subtle Pressure

Activity Level: 4   **Age Level: 9+**
Location: Inside or outside **Group Size: 2**

Game Description:
Partners face off. Player one puts their hand on player two's head and slowly presses down. Player two reacts to the pressure by sinking a bit. Then, slowly, player one's hand is lighter and player two feels herself pulled up. Do it a few times and switch roles.

Special Hints:
This is a subtle and sensitive game, best done with people who are caring for one another or who might be caring if given the chance.

Circuits

Activity Level: 4   **Age Level: 8+**
Location: Inside or outside   **Group Size: 8**

Game Description:
All players in a circle. Pass hand squeezes to the left saying "laa." Pass hand squeezes to the right saying "maa."

Variations:
Add and subtract movements and sounds according to abilities.

Special Hints:
A subtle game of coordination. Can evolve with the children.

Guess Our Shape

Activity Level: 4   **Age Level: 4+**
Location: Inside or outside   **Group Size: 4**

Game Description:
Children divide into two groups. One group decides on a shape to imitate, such as a crocodile or an ice cream cone, using every person in the group. The other group must guess what it is or get close. Then it is the other group's turn.

Special Hints:
Creates a peaceful atmosphere.

Body Ball

Activity Level: 4   **Age Level: 4+**
Location: Inside or outside   **Group Size: 2**
Materials: Beach ball

Game Description:
Without using hands, partners try to get a beach ball from the ground to their heads.

Variations:
Other size balls. More players.

Special Hints:
A good way to let children who are having difficulty with one another be together.

Alphabet

Activity Level: 4   **Age Level: 7+**
Location: Inside or outside   **Group Size: 10**

Game Description:
Each player becomes one or more letters of the alphabet, then they have to form words.

Variations:
Time the children. Name a theme. Make a sentence.

Special Hints:
Good for teaching spelling, etc. Can be combined with animal games.

Direct Me

Activity Level: 4
Location: Inside or outside
Materials: Rock and blindfold

Age Level: 3+
Group Size: 4

Game Description:

Children stand in a circle, with one in the middle blindfolded. Place the rock on the floor. Circle tries to direct blindfolded player to step on the rock.

Variations:

Vary sophistication of directions allowed. Blindfold partners.

Special Hints:

Good way to teach directions to young children.

Getting Together

Activity Level: 4
Location: Inside

Age Level: 5+
Group Size: 15

Game Description:

Count off by ones, twos, and threes. Everyone walks around shaking hands with whomever they meet. Ones shake once, twos give two shakes and so on. When they find someone with the same number they hold hands until all of the same numbers are joined.

Special Hints:

A good way to form teams.

Hello

Activity Level: 4   **Age Level: 3+**
Location: Inside or outside   **Group Size: 12**

Game Description:
Players stand in a circle. Each person attempts to make eye contact with another. Once contact is established those players change places.

Variations:
Add greetings. Funny things to do or say during switching. Add music. Hand clapping of syllables in name as it is spoken.

Special Hints:
Excellent icebreaker. Make sure everyone is included.

Where Is It?

Activity Level: 4   **Age Level: 6+**
Location: Inside or outside   **Group Size: 7**
Materials: Pebble

Game Description:
In a circle, with one player in the middle whose eyes are closed. Others pass the pebble. The one in the middle opens eyes and tries to guess who has the stone. Others keep passing it or pretend they are passing it. The pebble must always be in motion. Passes and fakes go on in both directions but always between persons next to one another.

Special Hints:
Encourage good fakery.

Huh?

Activity Level: 4   **Age Level: 5+**
Location: Inside   **Group Size: 2**

Game Description:
Partners talk together without using words. They have to make up sounds that make no sense to them and carry on a conversation.

Variations:
Make the sounds in rhythm to do group poetry. Act out a theme. Do movement and sounds. Have some children guess what the others are doing.

Special Hints:
One of the best for teaching communication.

Mime Rhyme

Activity Level: 4   **Age Level: 8+**
Location: Inside   **Group Size: 4+**

Game Description:
Player thinks up a word and tells others a word that rhymes with it. Others try to guess the word, but must act out their guess in pantomime. Player tells whether that guess is right.

Special Hints:
Good for new groups, for rainy days, and for improving communication.

Human Puzzles

Activity Level: 4   **Age Level: 4+**
Location: Inside   **Group Size: 5**
Materials: Homemade puzzle pieces

Game Description:
In groups of 5 to 7, each child is given a piece of a puzzle. Working together, they put the puzzle together.

Variations:
Increase complexity. Let group puzzles fit together to make one large puzzle. Let each group make up a story about their puzzle. Let each story be a chapter in the class story puzzle.

Chalkboard Drawing

Activity Level: 4   **Age Level: 4+**
Location: Inside   **Group Size: 15**
Materials: Chalk and chalkboard

Game Description:
Children draw circles on chalkboard under various handicaps, for instance in opposite direction with each hand; blindfolded; with objects on the back of the hand.

Variations:
Change shapes. Change drawing tool (e.g., chalk held in a clothespin). Work a theme.

Special Hints:
Keep the focus on well-drawn shapes. Helps individuals reentering.

Feel and Find Boxes

Activity Level: 4
Location: Inside
Age Level: 5+
Group Size: 1
Materials: Anything and everything

Game Description:

A box is constructed with a curtain on the front. Various objects are placed in it which the children try to guess by touch.

Variations:

Change box size. Change objects. Place duplicates on top for matching. Use objects from nature.

Special Hints:

Increase complexity continually.

Activity Level 5

Dilemmas

Activity Level: 5   **Age Level:** 10+
Location: Inside or outside   **Group Size:** 6+
Materials: Several ethical dilemmas, printed out
(samples below)

Game Description:

Sit with students. Hand out the ethical dilemmas (one to each student). Students can work individually or in small groups.

Give them 10 minutes to plan (or discuss if in a small group) how they would handle the dilemma they were given.

After 10 minutes, each person or group describes how they would go about resolving their dilemma.

Briefly discuss each response before moving on to the next group.

Variations:

Have the players come up with their own dilemmas.

Special Hints:

Co-create safety with players. Ask players to agree on some ground rules. Add to these safety rules as needed. For example, no right or wrong answers, no judgments of one another, no interruptions of the speaker.

Carefully observe, as some players may become annoyed with others. Use inquiry to help players explore how they came to their decisions for safety. If players are in small groups, multiple opinions for each group are fine. Make sure shy people are heard.

Check your own biases so they don't interfere with facilitation.

Sample Dilemmas:

#1 — You are a teacher. You have a student who is from a single-parent family. The student must work to earn enough money to attend college. However, the job is interfering with the student's performance in their studies, and several assignments have not been turned in. You have determined that the student has earned the grade of "D." Then the counselor informs you that the student needs a grade of "C" to qualify for an academic scholarship. What do you do?

#2 — Julia's best friend has turned against her and is now organizing the other girls to bully and isolate Julia. What can Julia do?

#3 — A fifth grade boy is overcome with hurt and anger when a classmate spreads a lie about him.

#4 — Three of Deziré's classmates have created an offensive website that attacks other students and teachers. The principal wants to know who created this website. Deziré is the only one who knows who did it. Should she lie to the principal or tell the truth, which would betray her classmates?

#5 — Amirah cringes every time she hears her friends use words like *retarded* or *gay* in a derogatory manner. Should she object when it happens, or should she let it pass so people won't think she's weird?

#6 — Someone left money sticking out of an ATM machine, and there's nobody in sight. Nobody but Ben, that is. If he takes it, does that make him a thief? What should he do?

#7 — Diego has just joined a Facebook group, and he discovers that somebody has posted an offensive and malicious photo of a girl from his class. Diego feels very uncomfortable about it. What, if anything, should he do?

Culture Creation in a Box

This activity can be done at an extended family retreat, in a family meeting, or within a classroom of 8- to 12-year-old students.

Activity Level: 5 **Age Level: 9+**
Location: Inside **Group Size: 7+**
Materials: Valentine's Day heart-shaped candy box (without the candy) or similar, red-colored card stock, marking pens, large piece of red tissue paper, double-sided sticky tape.

Preparation ahead of time (for the facilitator):

- Write (or print) the values listed below on pieces of card stock.
- Cut out each value into a small oval card. Put all the values cards into the heart-shaped box.
- Cut a big red heart out of poster board (approx. 26" × 36"). After the activity is completed, this big red heart will go on the wall (with double-sided sticky tape), and the values selected by the group will be displayed.

Game Description:

Everyone sits on the floor or rug together. Put the heart-shaped box in the middle.

Read the instructions aloud and ad lib wherever you want to tailor it to your group.

Instructions to read to all participants:

- Our hearts keep us alive.
- Some say the heart is where all our *goodness* lives.

Can anyone tell me what *values* mean? (Let the participants respond. Don't correct; just take the best of what is offered, put it together, and add to it as you see fit.)

Together we will select the values that are really important to us. These are the things that you really value and care about a lot. Pick values that you feel will keep your relationships special and alive. These must be things that are really important for you and your relationships. We will put these values on the heart.

Sometimes there are things that we feel really hinder relationships. These things can ruin friendships or can harm what is really important to us. Let's put those things into two piles outside the heart: (1) to be discussed later and (2) to be discarded. (Everyone must agree on the ones that get discarded completely.)

Activity:

Open the box and spread the values all around on the floor, rug, or very large table. Have the large heart nearby, also on the floor, rug, or table.

Allow each person to take turns to select a value they feel is important to include. The person whose turn it is will say why they want that value. Everyone votes. Then that value will get stuck to the heart (with the tape).

These become the ethos of the culture, whether a classroom, an extended family retreat, or a family meeting.

If everyone cannot agree on a selected value, that one can go into a pile marked "To be discussed later." This discussion can take place later in the event or can happen at a future time.

The values that are not selected can be discussed or they be can discarded entirely if everyone agrees.

It works best if there are no compromises such as agreeing to disagree.

HONESTY

CARING

We care for each other.

LYING
Lying is OK if you lie if you get away with it.

FAIRNESS

TATTLING
If you knew your friend was going to do something unsafe,
it is ok for you tell someone about it, even though you
promised you wouldn't.

BREAKING PROMISES
It's ok to break a promise you made.

DEPENDABILITY
You should always do what you say and say what you do.

DO WHAT I SAY
It is fair when an adult tells you that you can't do
something that they do because they are the adult.

ADULTS KNOW BEST
Adults always know what is best for kids.

INSPIRATION

TEASING IS OK

FRIENDSHIP
Friends are important.

TRUTH
It's important to always tell the truth to a teacher.

JEALOUSY
Jealousy is natural — everyone feels jealous sometimes.

CONSEQUENCES ARE OK
The direct effect of an action that provides an
opportunity for learning — the goal is to learn from
mistakes, take responsibility, and make better choices.

LOVE
Knowing we love each other is the most important thing.

FIGHTING
Fighting and hitting as a way to express
your emotions is OK.

PUNISHMENT
Sometimes it's OK for teachers to punish kids.

EQUALITY
All classmates should be equal.

FAIRNESS
It's important that we try to be fair.

LISTENING
It's important that we try to listen to one another.

ADVENTURE
We need to go on adventures together — unusual, wild,
exciting, and inspirational experiences.

FEELINGS
Talking about feelings is important.

CEREMONIES

CHORES
Chores can be fun if you do them together.

TELEVISION
No television when you first wake up.

CULTURE
Different cultures are part of who we are.

HONOR
Honor is important.

KEEPING YOUR WORD

NO PUT DOWNS

PRIDE
We are proud to be who we are.

JOKING AND LAUGHING
These are important in our class.

COMMUNICATION
Talking things through is important.

TIME FOR FUN TOGETHER

SPIRITUALITY

COMMUNITY

INTEGRITY

ACCOUNTABILITY
Each person is responsible for their own actions.

RESPECT

EMPATHY
Feel another person's feelings.

Watch My Face

Activity Level: 5   **Age Level: 4+**
Location: Inside or outside   **Group Size: 8**

Game Description:
Players stand in a circle. One player starts a crazy face one way. When that one is going she starts another one going the other way. When it makes the round someone else begins.

Variations:
Add a sound.

Try Not to Laugh

Activity Level: 5
Location: Inside or outside
Age Level: 4+
Group Size: 4

Game Description:
Players sit in a circle. One is It, and calls "Muk." This ends all conversation and smiling. It is now up to the one who is It to make another talk or smile. Anything goes, but no touching and no averting eyes.

Special Hints:
Play along. Introduce surprise. A good way to calm things down.

What Did I Do?

Activity Level: 5
Location: Inside or outside
Age Level: 6+
Group Size: 2

Game Description:
Partners face off. Player A examines player B for a minute or two and then turns her back. Player B changes five things about her appearance. Player A turns around and tries to guess what has been changed.

Variations:
Vary the time of observation and the amount of things changed. Do it with an area and not a person.

Special Hints:
Help out those who get stumped. Don't let it become competitive.

Where Did It Go?

Activity Level: 5   **Age Level: 5+**
Location: Inside   **Group Size: 6**
Materials: Small bell, blindfold

Game Description:
One player sits in the middle, blindfolded. The other players pass a bell around with each player ringing it once. They stop and the last one puts it behind her back. The one in the center tries to guess where it is.

Webs

Activity Level: 5   **Age Level: 5+**
Location: Inside or outside   **Group Size: 5**
Materials: Ball of yarn

Game Description:
Using a big ball of yarn, hold the end and toss the ball to another. All are seated in a circle. The player with the yarn gets to speak to the group. While holding onto the yarn end, pass the ball to another player (randomly) in the circle. Watch the web form.

Variations:
Introduce a theme on which all have to speak.

Special Hints:
Allow the option to pass without speaking. Play fairly regularly for group solidarity. Let important issues arise.

Nature Web

Activity Level: 5 **Age Level: 8+**
Location: Inside or outside **Group Size: 5**
Materials: Ball of yarn

Game Description:

Holding a ball of yarn the leader asks the first child to name a plant. The ball of yarn is thrown to player 1. Then ask: "What animal eats that plant?" The ball is thrown to the second player, 2, with player 1 holding the end. Then ask: "What animal eats that animal?" The yarn is thrown to player 3. Then: "Where does that animal live?" and so on until a web representing the local ecology is formed. Then introduce a plausible disaster. Tug on the point of the web that represented that part of the environment that would be destroyed. Who else feels the tug? And so on.

Special Hints:

Here's safe space for everyone to communicate their values concerning the environment.

Dictionary

Activity Level: 5   **Age Level: 10**
Location: Inside   **Group Size: 5**
Materials: Dictionary; pencils; paper

Game Description:
One player picks a strange word from the dictionary. She writes it down on a slip of paper. She says the word. Everyone else writes down a definition for the word. Then the definitions are read aloud and everyone tries to guess which one was right.

Variations:
Try to guess who wrote which definition.

Special Hints:
Great for vocabulary building. Can be great fun for leaders.

T-Shirts

Activity Level: 5   **Age Level: 4+**
Location: Inside   **Group Size: 6**
Materials: T-shirt outline on a piece of paper; scissors; drawing tools

Game Description:
Give each child a piece of paper with a T-shirt outline on it. Let them cut the shirt out and write their name in the middle. Then ask them questions about their life and values and have them write or draw the answers on various parts of the shirt.

Variations:
Examples: favorite animal, place in home, or memory.

Special Hints:
Allow time for decorating. Excellent for insight into values. Builds self-esteem.

ReConnect

Activity Level: 5   **Age Level: 5+**
Location: Inside or outside   **Group Size: 2**

Game Description:
Eyes closed, partners face off, touch palms, feel the energy, and drop arms. Then take two steps back, turn three times, and try to reconnect palms.

Variations:
Bend arms and try to touch agreed upon other body parts. Do it in a circle.

Special Hints:
It's fun to watch, so make it a group activity even if only two are playing.

Guess

Activity Level: 5   **Age Level: 4+**
Location: Inside   **Group Size: 5+**
Materials: Weird handheld objects and a sheet

Game Description:
Players sit in a circle with sheet covering hands and lower arms. Weird object is passed around under the sheet and everyone tries to guess what it is.

Variations:
Choose object suitable to level of players.

Special Hints:
Let little ones feel first before guessing. Guess in turn and don't reveal until the end. Or, guess silently so no one feels left out.

Casual Conversation

Activity Level: 5 **Age Level: 8+**
Location: Inside or outside **Group Size: 6**

Game Description:

The group sends two people out of earshot and decides on two different sentences. The pair is called back and each is privately told one of the sentences. The pair proceeds to have a "conversation." Each tries to insert their sentence into the conversation before the other. If the other speaker suspects the sentence has been said, she can challenge. Each player is allowed three challenges. When the sentence is either challenged correctly or passes undetected, the game is over and two new players go.

Special Hints:

Younger children will need some coaching at first. Remind them to develop conversation before attempting to insert their sentence. Sample sentences: "When salmon spawn they turn bright red." Or "Human beings have 40 million brain cells." Good game to pair children who don't often talk to each other or play together. With care, it serves to pair children who don't get along.

Silent Drawing

Activity Level: 5　　　　　**Age Level: 4+**
Location: Inside　　　　　**Group Size: 2**
Materials: Drawing tools; painting tools; large sheets of paper

Game Description:
Two players hold the same brush or crayon and draw on the same piece of paper. No talking.

Variations:
Have several pairs draw on the same piece of paper. Let one pair finish before the next begins. Suggest a theme.

Special Hints:
Vary partners. Encourage slow starters.

Do You Know Me?

Activity Level: 5　　　　　**Age Level: 4+**
Location: Inside or outside　　**Group Size: 8**
Materials: Blindfold

Game Description:
A blindfolded player is led to the group sitting in a line or semicircle. She is told to identify one person in the group by gently touching everyone's face, one by one, until she finds who she is looking for. After she guesses, the blindfold is removed and another player goes.

Variations:
Identification by touching hands only. Identify each person as they are touched.

Special Hints:
Only touch face, not clothing or jewelry. Silence is critical.

Silent Structures

Activity Level: 5   **Age Level: 6+**
Location: Inside   **Group Size: 4**
Materials: Colored paper; masking tape; scissors

Game Description:
Divide children into groups of 4 to 6. Give each group two pairs of scissors, two rolls of masking tape and a stack of colored paper. One color per group. Tell the children to build a castle. No talking allowed.

Variations:
Allow talking. Use random materials at hand.
Limit resources: limit of 1 yard of masking tape per group.

Special Hints:
Hold a discussion afterwards to bring out decision-making role of each child. Vary group makeup. Builds nonverbal communication skills.

Cooperative House Play

Activity Level: 5   **Age Level: 3+**
Location: Inside or outside   **Group Size: 2**
Materials: Varies

Game Description:
Work around the house can be turned into a cooperative adventure. Cooking can be done with only one hand, or with only one person knowing the recipe and no talking allowed. Gardening can also be done under similar handicaps to promote cooperation.

Variations:
Limited only by your imagination.

Special Hints:
Approach with good humor and no time limit.

Lion, Fox, Deer, Dove

Activity Level: 5 **Age Level: 7+**
Location: Inside **Group Size: 12**
Materials: Four pieces of poster board and a marker

Game Description:
Make a poster board sign each for Lion, Fox, Deer, and Dove. Ask the players to go to the animal that they most resemble and join the group. Let them discuss among themselves why they picked that animal. Then a spokesperson from each group explains to everyone the feelings and thoughts of her animal group.

Variations:
Pick other animals or issues to discuss.

Special Hints:
The discussion is critical. It will reveal the predispositions of the players. This activity also promotes acceptance of diversity.

Prehistoric Communication

Activity Level: 5 **Age Level: 8+**
Location: Inside **Group Size: 4**
Materials: Paper and drawing tools

Game Description:
Form groups of 4. One from each group comes to the leader, who whispers a word in her ear. That person turns to the group and draws the word or phrase while the others try to guess. Then another player gets a new word.

Variations:
Two do the drawing holding one drawing tool, either communicating with one another or not. Can draw more than one picture.

Special Hints:
If it goes too long, the next person goes.

Cooperative Storytelling

Activity Level: 5   **Age Level: 3+**
Location: Inside or outside   **Group Size: 3**

Game Description:
Players make up a story one sentence at a time, with each player taking a turn, build on the previous sentence to enhance the story.

Variations:
Each player takes a paragraph. Introduce a theme. Leader takes the lead and keeps the theme alive.

Special Hints:
Encourage all to play. Excellent around a campfire. Can lead to collective picture.

Collage

Activity Level: 5   **Age Level: 5+**
Location: Inside   **Group Size: 4**
Materials: Glue; scissors; old magazines; poster board

Game Description:
A theme is introduced and the group collectively creates a collage.

Variations:
Any theme. Can make a group gift.

Special Hints:
Good for a rainy day.

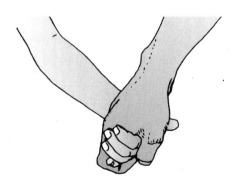

APPENDIX A

Natural Learning Relationships Overview

NATURAL LEARNING RELATIONSHIPS (NLR) is a practical and applicable whole-child developmental science. NLR details the psychological, emotional, physical, and spiritual components of optimal well-being. Furthermore, it describes the dynamics by which these capacities emerge within each stage of childhood. Relationship based, NLR includes the context of the child's life, family, school, and background. It is founded on both fieldwork and the literature in child development, family systems, and contiguous psychological disciplines.

Each stage of childhood has a unique purpose and unique needs. When the needs are satisfied, the purpose is fulfilled. When a child experiences that fulfillment their well-being reaches optimal levels. The child then has the best environment for social, emotional, physical, intellectual, and spiritual growth.

In order to encourage full capacity and potential in children, it is necessary for parents, caregivers, and teachers to value and understand the developmental stages of childhood. To fully comprehend the child, we must consider the whole child, inclusive of intellect; emotional, social, and physical development; and spiritual nature. This is development of the whole person (or whole being of the child).

Natural Learning Relationships offers detailed examination of transitions throughout childhood and suggestions as to how to nurture and support children through these often misunderstood yet critical times for growth, learning, and stability.

Life stages contain capacities, but development occurs *in relationship*. Based on our extensive research and work in the field of holistic education and family empowerment, we believe that Natural Learning Relationships is the only approach to development that acknowledges the relationships among all parties (child as well as adult) and determines the quality of development for all. Successful fulfillment in each life stage means that everyone grows together.

Natural Learning Relationships specifically delineates the psychological and emotional nourishments for each life stage as well as optimal environments that support children's innate capacities. At the same time, Natural Learning Relationships helps educators find a way to provide these nourishments that is in accord with their school culture, lifestyle, environment, economic condition, unique family values, and individual needs. In this way Natural Learning Relationships supports diversity and universal access while providing a map to well-being for all children and their caregivers.

Key Attributes of Each Developmental Stage

BODYBEING Children	
Ages: 0 through 7 years (depending on the child and the environment)	
Organizing Principle (OP)	**1st OP** — Rightful place, secure attachment, and belonging **2nd OP** — Boundaries and personal strength
Language	**Sensory-based communication:** Children at this age primarily experience the world through their sensory explorations.
Key Nourishment	**Loving touch with an attitude of acceptance:** People who are affectionate and lovingly touch with an attitude of acceptance.
Secondary Nourishment	Security, warmth, nourishment, and flexibility
Meaning-Making Moment	At approximately 2½ or 3 years of age, a new ability to use language symbolically appears. Simultaneously children engage more complex communication and creativity in both discovering and ascribing meaning in their world.
Hindrance to Development	**Perceived physical threat:** Anything which threatens the child's sense of security.
Well-Being Attributes of BodyBeing Children	I know I am loved, wanted, and cared for. I feel secure in my family and connected. I have a place in the world. I know my boundaries and can explore my world safely.

FEELINGBEING Children	
Ages: 8 through 12 (depending on the child and the context)	
Organizing Principle	1st **OP** — Trust 2nd **OP** — Reciprocal cooperation
Language	**Feelings and emotions:** Honest information about feelings
Key Nourishment	**Feeling mentors:** Elders who are able to share feelings honestly, without an ulterior motive, speak the language of feelings and remember that the child is always feeling. Be honest about mistakes.
Secondary Nourishment	Fairness, relationship, caring, adventure, honesty, adaptability, and justice
Meaning-Making Moment	At approximately 10½ years of age, awareness expands, which precipitates a search for information about that which lies beyond physical life and which often expresses itself in experiences of transcendence. There seems to be a relationship between opening in awareness and feelings of religious devotion generated from within the child, not as a consequence of externally imposed morality.
Hindrance to Development	**Hypocrisy:** Insincerity, falseness, pretending to have qualities that are not there. The goal is not perfection; rather, it is all about a working relationship to Truth.
Well-Being Attributes of FeelingBeing Children	I trust my own goodness so I can make mistakes and learn from them. I trust myself and those around me to be honest and caring about feelings. I engage and cooperate with people.

IDEABEING Teenagers Ages: 13 through 17 (depending on the child and the environment)	
Organizing Principle	1st OP—Healthy autonomy: the ability to self-govern in a healthy way and uncover their own core nature 2nd OP—Identity construction, freedom with responsibility matrix, social ability with right relationship to personal power
Language	**Inquiry into the teen's ideals**
Key Nourishment	**Sensitive respect:** Support for the child's search for identities that express core nature
Secondary Nourishment	Adventure, energetic activities, peer sensitivity, self-designed challenges within the realm of success, identity exploration opportunities, opportunities to express their ideals and work with them
Meaning-Making Moment	At approximately 15 years of age, teens experience the clarity of their ideals along with a movement toward creating their own identity (that matches their core nature). Teens also explore their newfound personal power and a desire for more freedom. Teens see the potential greatness of things that can be done in the world and recognize that their identity can be part of and contribute to that greatness. Meaning feeds into their identity choices.
Hindrance to Teen Development	**Ridicule:** Disrespects with derision the teen's identity explorations. Ridicule emphasizes the teen's insecurity and kills self-esteem, which hurts open social explorations.
Well-Being Attributes of Healthy Teenagers	I can self-govern and make healthy choices. I have organized an identity that can express my ideals. I can navigate a wide variety of social environments confidently. I am resilient and am able to act responsibly with freedom I am given.

REASONABLEBEING Individuals Ages: 18 through 23 (depending on the environment)	
Organizing Principle	**1st OP** — Substantive values (that endure through time), interconnectedness, humor, and humility matrix **2nd OP** — Purpose and meaning, to act with intentionality and incisiveness, relationship (with commitment through time), and the ability to discern and discriminate
Language	**Dialog into meaning** — toward reasonable logic
Key Nourishment	**Mature recognition:** Acknowledgment of the child's equality, achievements, abilities for commitment, and the ability for recognition of self
Secondary Nourishment	Comparison, recapitulation, inquiry, exploration, experimentation, suggestion, investigation, discernment
Meaning-Making Moment	At 18 or 19 years of age, the awesome and humbling experience of the vastness and mystery underlying all life is cognitively accepted. This includes a greatly expanded appreciation of time and space. The search for the depth of meaning arises and begs to be answered. All values are scrutinized for their eternal qualities.
Hindrance to Development	**Condescension:** Hinders relationship and stops reasonableness. The individual moves toward self-protection (defensiveness), and communication closes down.
Well-Being Attributes of ReasonableBeing Individuals	I have a sense of enduring values. My life has purpose, meaning, and direction. I understand my past and can act in the present to create the future I want. I make commitments that I keep over time. I can communicate with others and make meaning together to create a better social world.

Glossary of Terms

- **Language:** Each stage of childhood has its own mode of communication. To effectively communicate with any age child, one must speak the language of their developmental stage.

- **Meaning Making:** A frame of reference that we create from past experiences and use to interpret new experience. Meaning perspectives are rule systems of habitual expectations and schemes (knowledge, beliefs, value judgments, and feelings) that make up our habitual set of expectations and assumptions. Meaning perspectives influence the way we define, understand, and act in a new experience.

  Each developmental stage has a meaning-making moment during which the information that has been received during the beginning years of the stage synergistically burst forth into a new ordering of the world.

- **Nourishment:** The psychological, social, emotional, and physical environments that truly nurture the Organizing Principle for well-being in each developmental stage. Important for all children, nourishment means to provide the food and environments necessary for life and growth. Thus, diet, health maintenance, and learning tools (such as toys), educational materials, and play environments are all forms of nourishment. Moreover, the adult's psychological attitudes toward the child are part of that child's environment.

- **Organizing Principle:** The force that determines the general ways in which human energy, capacities, inclinations, and interactions are structured and act. The goal of each OP is well-being, and the energy, capacities, inclinations, and interactions it has to work with are developmentally and contextually bound. Each OP takes the qualities, capacities, and talents of the relevant age group and uses them to promote the well-being of the children. Each OP changes to suit children's development in each successive stage of development.

- **Well-Being:** A dynamically balanced state of health, which optimizes our opportunities for self-actualization. This view suggests that people who possess well-being also have adaptive abilities, life-satisfaction, a sense of personal meaning in life, insights, sound judgment, and the ability to amplify the positive effects of emotional awareness and intelligence. In a state of well-being, people have the highest potential to access wisdom.

- **Whole-Child:** All aspects of the individual child (e.g., physical, psychological, intelligence, emotional, spiritual aspects) and the interdependence of all the parts. It is not concerned with reducing children into parts and then analyzing each part.

- **Wisdom:** Qualities of wisdom include, but are not limited to, the right actions according to the context of a person's present developmental moment in his or her life. Moreover, we each have an inherent source of wisdom — an *inner wisdom* — that provides us with opportunities to experience life, to learn and grow, and to actualize our individual and collective destinies.

- **Wisdom-Based Relationship:** In wisdom-based relationships we interact with children in a way that nurtures their Organizing Principle. In so doing, we activate deeper connection to our own Organizing Principle. In wisdom-based relationships there is mutual benefit, and each party grows in self-knowledge. Adults who nurture children's developmental needs (specific to each Organizational Principle) live in wisdom-based relationships with children.

Books about Cooperative Games

Cain, Jim and Barry Jolliff. *Teamwork & Teamplay*. Kendall/Hunt Publishing, 1998.

Cain, Jim and Tom Smith. *The Book on Raccoon Circles*. Learning Unlimited, 2002.

Gibbs, Jeanne. *Tribes: A New Way of Learning and Being Together*. Centersource Systems, 2001.

Lefevre, Dale N. *Best New Games: 77 Games and 7 Trust Activities for All Ages and Abilities*. Human Kinetics Publishers, 2001.

Luvmour, Sambhava and Josette Luvmour. *Win-Win Games for All Ages: Cooperative Activities for Building Social Skills*. New Society Publishers, 2002.

Rohnke, Karl E. *Silver Bullets: A Guide to Initiative Problems, Adventure Games and Trust Activities*. Kendall/Hunt Publishing, 1989. (Reprint edition)

Rohnke, Karl E. *Cowstails and Cobras: A Guide to Games, Initiatives, Ropes Courses and Adventure Curriculum*. Kendall/Hunt Publishing, 2003.

Sikes, Sam. *Raptor*. Kendall/Hunt Publishing, 1998.

Indices

Games Group Size Index
One or more players

Two or More Players

151

Three or More Players

Four or More Players

Five or More Players

Six or More Players

Seven or More Players

Eight or More Players

Games Age Level Index

Age One and Up

Age Three and Up

Age Four and Up

Age Five and Up

Age Six and Up

Age Nine and Up

About the Authors

*J*OSETTE AND BA LUVMOUR have lived, studied, worked, and played together since 1979. They are educators who have started several holistic education schools, a holistic learning center for families and children, and many whole-family immersion programs (in both California and Oregon).

Teachers of children and parents, they are also teachers of other teachers (undergrad and graduate master's students), many of whom went on to start their own schools in the USA and Canada using Natural Learning Relationships child development and holistic approaches in their teaching practice. They founded two nonprofit organizations dedicated to awakening the greatness in humanity.

Together, Josette and Ba co-created and developed Natural Learning Relationships, a holistic understanding of child development that supports optimal well-being in children and families. Natural Learning Relationships was the basis and philosophical foundation of the schools, learning center, and programs they founded as well as in their published work of six print books, five eBooks, and magazine and journal articles. They produce and host the popular podcast series, *Meetings with Remarkable Educators*.

Josette and Ba are continually inspired by all those who learn with children and *grow together* to access greater self-knowledge, well-being, and ultimately wisdom.

A Note about the Publisher

NEW SOCIETY PUBLISHERS is an activist, solutions-oriented publisher focused on publishing books for a world of change. Our books offer tips, tools, and insights from leading experts in sustainable building, homesteading, climate change, environment, conscientious commerce, renewable energy, and more — positive solutions for troubled times.

We're proud to hold to the highest environmental and social standards of any publisher in North America. This is why some of our books might cost a little more. We think it's worth it!

- We print all our books in North America, never overseas
- All our books are printed on **100% post-consumer recycled paper**, processed chlorine free, with low-VOC vegetable-based inks (since 2002)
- Our corporate structure is an innovative employee shareholder agreement, so we're one-third employee-owned (since 2015)
- We're carbon-neutral (since 2006)
- We're certified as a B Corporation (since 2016)

At New Society Publishers, we care deeply about *what* we publish — but also about *how* we do business.

Download our catalogue at https://newsociety.com/Our-Catalog or for a printed copy please email info@newsocietypub.com or call 1-800-567-6772 ext 111

New Society Publishers
ENVIRONMENTAL BENEFITS STATEMENT

For every 5,000 books printed, New Society saves the following resources:[1]

16	Trees
1,462	Pounds of Solid Waste
1,609	Gallons of Water
2,098	Kilowatt Hours of Electricity
2,658	Pounds of Greenhouse Gases
11	Pounds of HAPs, VOCs, and AOX Combined
4	Cubic Yards of Landfill Space

[1]Environmental benefits are calculated based on research done by the Environmental Defense Fund and other members of the Paper Task Force who study the environmental impacts of the paper industry.

Certified
(B)
Corporation

MIX
Paper from responsible sources
FSC® C016245

new society
PUBLISHERS
www.newsociety.com